OUR
COLLEGE
STORY

A short history of the King's College
of St Nicholas and Our Lady in Cambridge

ROSS HARRISON
(Former Provost)

First published in 2015 by
King's College, Cambridge

Copyright © 2015 King's College, Cambridge

Reprinted 2022

A CIP Catalogue of this book is available from
the British Library

ISBN: 978-0-9934005-0-6

Typeset in 11½pt Bembo by
www.chandlerbookdesign.com

Printed in Great Britain by
CPI Antony Rowe,
Chippenham, Wiltshire

CONTENTS

The College expresses its grateful thanks to Ross Harrison, who undertook the writing of this book, and to Peter Jones, the College's Fellow Librarian, who has done so much to prepare the text for publication.

CHAPTER ONE

THE KING'S KING'S

S tarting his sonnet on King's College Chapel, William Wordsworth's well-worn words were "tax not the royal saint with vain expense." Nowadays not many people do and those responsible for the massive fabric dominating central Cambridge are inclined instead to wish that the royal saint had been vainer. Not that anyone would wish the Chapel larger, but rather that the saint had provided a larger endowment for its continuing support. In this chapter, I aim to explain the College's foundation. A certain shortage of initial endowment might be only to be expected from a founding saint; "high heaven," Wordsworth goes on to say, "rejects the lore of nicely-calculated less or more." But this particular chapel was built on earth. The building alone took seventy years of mundane struggle with less or more, chiefly less. Then, once the external fabric was completed, it has been maintained in its breath-taking beauty for a further five hundred years of low calculation. All done by the lore of less or more and, as will be seen, the royal founder was in fact more ambitious than would be indicated by what survives to be contemplated by poets and others; he wanted more built than there was and he intended more vain expense in its support than actually occurred.

Henry, King of England, sixth of that name, Henri, King of France, second of that name, Lord of Ireland and Duke of Aquitaine, founded King's College Cambridge by letters patent on 12 February 1441. Reasonably referred to as a royal saint, although never formally canonised, he might reasonably also be called a royal fiddler. He had plans; he fiddled; and then he had further plans. After they had started building his planned chapel at his simultaneous foundation at Eton, he decided to have it knocked down and done differently. After they had started building his planned college in Cambridge, he decided to found it again in a different place and with different purpose. And all through this decade of the 1440s he was actively engaged, fiddling with the plans. The King had advisers and the actual hard work was done by royal officials. But King Henry was personally engaged in what he himself called his first notable work. He oversaw the plans; he twice came in person to Cambridge to lay foundation stones; and his notable work expresses his personal, saintly, qualities.

Unfortunately these were not the qualities required for being a good king in the fifteenth century and in fact Henry was about as unsuccessful as it is possible to be as a king, or even as a person. His kingdom descended into civil war; he was defeated, captured, and passed around like a totemic parcel; he went mad several times; his only son was defeated and killed in battle; and he himself was murdered in the Tower of London. So King's and Eton were founded by a failure. Yet however salutary it may sometimes be to remind Eton of this unfortunate fact, each of the failure's foundations could robustly respond that the great deeds of more successful kings are now forgotten whereas King Henry's twin educational projects continue in rude health nearly six centuries after their foundation. And the success of the foundation is the founder's success.

Deciding to found a college in Cambridge meant the King's officers coming to Cambridge and purchasing property; changing all the plans meant them returning to Cambridge and buying much more property. And all this was not only planned by the supposedly saintly King but also all actually accomplished. It was only later that it all went wrong, for King, country, and also (as we shall see) for King's. The process started before the official foundation, when in 1440 a garden was bought from Trinity Hall. This was for operating Henry's first plan, which was for a small college near Trinity Hall with a Rector in charge and a few Fellows. His second plan, by letters patent of 10 July 1443, was instead to have a much larger college further south with a Provost in charge and many Fellows.

When King's was founded, there were other colleges but the University was the dominant force. The teaching was given by the University (in the form of disputations and lectures in the University Schools) and not by the colleges. The great majority of undergraduates were not members of colleges and the normal form of a college was a small corporation of more advanced scholars. All Souls College in Oxford has for centuries seemed like a strange anomaly in having only fellows but no undergraduates. But in fact it was the normal form of a college when it was founded shortly before the foundation of King's. Another important difference in the fifteenth century from what became natural later is the length of time that students engaged in study. Students worked in Cambridge for the full seven years for a Master's degree (instead of the later custom of heading off and doing nothing after the BA). So what we would now call graduate instruction was part of this medieval university. Even at this point, the course of honours was not complete. The scholar could specialise (normally in theology, but possibly also in canon or civil law, or medicine). Further possible years of organised study followed, leading to a bachelor's and then a doctoral degree in the speciality and it was these advanced scholars who conveniently combined in the colleges. They were generally in clerical orders; they were unmarried; and they lived more economically together both by sharing expenses but also by benefiting from the endowments provided by the college's founders and benefactors.

The final strand that needs to be added to this picture is the medium of instruction, which was Latin. So for any university in Europe, it would be the same: students could turn up from anywhere and receive instruction and attend disputations in the same single universal language. This meant that before students could attend university they had to be proficient in Latin; hence the importance of grammar schools (where 'grammar' meant that they taught Latin grammar). Students were expected to be able to speak and read Latin before arriving, putting pressure on the adequacy of the grammar schools. Shortly before King's was founded, a citizen of London founded a college specifically to educate the required grammar school masters. Unfortunately he put it in the wrong place; it got in the way of King Henry's second plan and had to be moved.

King Henry's first plan for a small college was standard, but his second plan was unprecedented in Cambridge in its size, its point, and its assumptions. It required a lot more land on which to build, a lot more buildings to put on this land, and much more money for both of these as well as to support many more people. Both buying and building take time and it was years before even the land needed for the second plan was acquired. The site that the King now wanted is the site on which the current college is built. So the good citizens of Cambridge had to be moved from a large part of the centre of their small town, on a site stretching from their High Street to the far side of their river, then the chief means of bringing in goods. The site had their private houses and also a college, student hostels, and a parish church. It had the lanes that they used to cross the town or get to the artery of the river, on the far side of which was their common. The Town granted to the King the roads, the common, and a quay known as Salthythe by the river. The citizens' houses were purchased piecemeal by the King's agents. But it was not until February 1449 that the whole site (apart from one draper, still holding out) could be delivered to the College by formal Act of King and Parliament.

We have the benefit of hindsight and so we know, unlike them, how long the King and College then had to make something of their newly acquired site. Six years later, the King was into civil war. Earlier, he had become deranged for a year, unable to speak or feed himself, lying in bed while others ran the country. He was finally deposed when Edward of York took over as King Edward IV in 1461. So there was no time at all to build a large college, or to fulfil Henry's plan before it lost its chief backer and motive support. There is a rather touching story (at least according to the then Provost) how when Henry was captured at the First Battle of St Albans in 1455, he begged his captors to continue with King's. They had other things to do and Henry did briefly regain his liberty and renew hope. But after his supporters were badly defeated and largely killed at the Battle of Towton in 1461, neither he nor the College had a further chance.

The Founder therefore cleared a large part of central Cambridge, leaving a massive building site and a hope. Eventually, the hope was realised and a college built on the site. But it took centuries and there are still large areas of open grass standing strangely in the centre of a city. The Founder's own very detailed plan for what to do with the new site was most fully set out in his so called 'Will' of 12 March 1448. Here he specifies the dimensions of his planned new chapel, much as were later achieved. Here he gives the dimensions of his planned 'quadrant' south of the chapel, again much as were later achieved in the present Front Court. However this court not only took 400 years to complete, as compared with Henry's planned 20, but is in a very different form. Henry's King's would have been like the later John's and Trinity, with a chapel on the north side of a fully enclosed front court of joined together buildings on all four sides (as opposed to the present detached buildings and open screen on one side). In Henry's plan, the hall and library would have been where the Gibbs Building now is together with "a large house for reading and disputations" under the library; the Provost's lodgings were to be in the court's south-west corner. Where the back lawn now is, there was to be a smaller court to the south, including the kitchens, and to the north of it a large cemetery and tower. None of this was ever built apart from the chapel, although there were burials on the site of the planned cemetery.

The Will sets out in equally exact detail how the building was to be financed. £1,000 a year was to be paid for twenty years from the Duchy of Lancaster, which was part of the King's personal possessions, and provision made in case more was needed after that. Trustees were appointed to see that it all happened. Here, as in the building descriptions, it can be seen that the 'Will' is not like a modern will: it gave the King's 'will' (or intention) as to what should happen in his life rather than what he wanted to happen after his death. But it also, like a modern will, included death, covering what was to happen if Henry died before the project was completed: King's and Eton were to be made the first call on the profits of the Duchy of Lancaster. From all this it can be seen how important these twin projects were to King Henry and how apparently unbreakable was the plan by which the projects would be accomplished. It had the King behind it; it was all tied up; it couldn't possibly go wrong. Yet, as we have also seen, in a few short years it got lost in madness, deposition, and war.

Required finance for new colleges is in two parts. Money is needed for building, as was planned in the 'Will'. But money is also needed for continuing expenses. So King's, like the other colleges, needed an endowment that provided an annual income. At that date, endowment was in land and King Henry through this same decade of the 1440s transferred estates to support his new re-founded college. Many were subsequently lost but some remained to which the Provost and Bursar travelled annually through the subsequent centuries, collecting rents from distant estates. The College was Lord of the Manor and so they also sat when they visited as the manorial court. And the College presented to the livings (that is, nominated the Rector or Vicar). So cleric after cleric moved after being a Fellow of King's to being Vicar of Ringwood in Hants, or Broad Chalke in Wilts, or Prescot in Lancs, or Rector of Stour Provost in Dorset; these names are woven for centuries through the fabric of the College and they all arrived in the 1440s.

So far we have a physical and a financial plan for the new college. Equally important is its constitution, as set out in its Statutes. Like the other things, these were provided by the Founder (written by others but personally approved by the King). Also like the other things, they don't form a single plan with a once given single set of Statutes but were again a changing process with several successive forms. The final set, which governed the College for the next 400 years (as 'The Founder's Statutes'), date from the 1450s. But these 1450s Statutes are not much different from those provided by the King in 1446, when he laid out the chief elements of his new plan for his re-founded college. The most important feature, which framed the essence of King's for centuries and made it radically different from any other Cambridge college, is Henry's plan to combine his two new foundations into a single project. University education, as we have seen, presupposed working knowledge of Latin, which presupposed a good prior grammar school education. Henry had in Eton such a school, newly designed to provide the very best education at this level anywhere in the country. So the heart of his second plan for King's was to take these already well trained boys and give them the very best university education that the country could supply to complement and complete the process. Boys were selected to be King's Scholars at Eton, where they were freely boarded, fed, and educated. They were then selected to come to King's, where again they were freely boarded and fed as Scholars. After three years, and so a year before they graduated, Scholars became Fellows; for centuries at King's all undergraduates in their final year were already Fellows. After graduating and already secure as Fellows, they could continue in the same supported way through as much of the courses described above as they wished, proceeding to MAs and then on to the higher degrees in law, medicine, or divinity; they could study for decades, or for life, free of financial considerations. King Henry's endowment to his twin colleges provided the income, and the income was used to provide a high level of education.

The Fellows freely fed in the college hall and freely lived in the college accommodation, as well as receiving an annual supply of clothing and payment in cash, only if they kept their Fellowships. By the Founder's Statutes, these could be lost on three grounds, in addition to expulsion for bad behaviour. The system was meant for 'poor scholars', so someone gaining an estate which would support him had to resign. So also someone presented to a 'living', that is to a paid ecclesiastical position such as the Vicar or Rector of a parish. The third ground requiring resignation was matrimony. In future centuries, the third and second ground often went together. A Fellow decided to marry and so moved out of the Fellowship and into a parish. Or he moved into a parish and, missing the company of the College, decided to marry. But medieval clergy were not married and so these were disjoint causes of resignation: some Fellows who became priests decided to move unmarried to parishes; some who stayed as laymen decided to marry and move out. The first cause of resignation (inheriting an estate) was less frequent than either of these, given that the King's Scholars at Eton were rarely from noble or gentry families. But it did happen.

One thing that helped change Henry's mind between his first and second plan was a visit to Winchester. Partly it got him thinking big on churches, with a massively spectacular large second design for his chapels at Eton and Cambridge. But he also, more particularly, picked up this idea of linking school and university. Eton and King's as a unified project imitates William Wykeham's plan of some forty years earlier when, as Bishop of Winchester, he founded a school at Winchester and linked it to a new college (aka 'New College') in Oxford. The Statutes are in part copied from this foundation and Henry imported the head of Winchester to get Eton going. In July 1444, as another significant event in this formative decade, the four colleges signed a treaty of mutual protection, known as the 'Amicabilis Concordia'. Although it didn't help any of them in the rough times that followed, it is still happily remembered, toasted, and specially celebrated on anniversaries.

Statutes are an internal system of law and the Founder matched the close control that this provided by exempting the College almost completely from any external control. He sought and received bulls from the Pope making the College completely independent of any external ecclesiastical jurisdiction, not just from the local bishop in Ely but also from the Archbishop of Canterbury. The College was also to have a peculiar independent status in the University, exempted from the jurisdiction of the Vice Chancellor. It was all too much for the first Provost, William Millington. He had been imported (probably from Clare) to take control of a small college across the street as its Rector. The place had then been re-founded as a much larger college further south and he had been translated into being Provost. So far, so good; indeed he had lobbied for something larger. But he hadn't signed up for a college completely composed of Etonians and he thought that the exemption from University jurisdiction was incompatible with his previous oath of loyalty to the Vice Chancellor. He protested and had to go, being replaced by the more pliable Chedworth, who smoothly managed to move on to being Bishop of Lincoln before the trouble started, happily hunting heretics and helping to stiffen up this aspect of the College Statutes.

As Bishop of Lincoln, John Chedworth was still in connection with the College as its Visitor because another aspect of the unification with Eton was to give King's the same visitor as Eton already had (and, implausible as it may seem, the diocese of Lincoln then extended as far south as Eton.) Another unifying element was changing the dedication. Eton was dedicated to Our Lady and indeed was founded in Eton so that it could take over the church of Our Lady of Eton as a place of pilgrimage. So King's was now also dedicated to Our Lady, acquiring a second saint to join its original founding saint, St Nicholas. All this and very much more is in the Founder's Statutes, which have a strange obsession with secrecy; any Fellow or Provost revealing the Statutes to outsiders was to be severely punished. Those in the know would discover that they circumscribed the smallest details of the life in College by both Scholars and Fellows, such as what they had to wear, when and how they could leave the College, the services for different days in chapel, and so on. Bible readings were prescribed not just in chapel but also while eating in hall, just as in a monastery. And, supporting the Latinate culture of a medieval university, when these readings stopped, the conversation during dinner had to be in Latin (unless strangers were present or what were called cases of necessity).

All this careful planning of people's lives would only work if there was money to pay for them and they had somewhere to live. They needed a hall in which to be read to while eating, a chapel for the statutory services, and so on. Not so easy with nothing more than ownership of a large empty chunk of devastated central Cambridge. But in fact, although the idea on which it was based had been superseded, the building that had started with Henry's first foundation was still continuing. Indeed it could be said of King Henry's two successive King's Colleges in Cambridge that the first was built but not planned and the second was planned but not built; he was that kind of king. In 1441, the date of the original foundation, work started on the land acquired from Trinity Hall with a gate tower across the street from it and Clare. Its position is still marked by what is currently the gatehouse to the Old Schools and the still existing court inside gives a very rough indication of size of the King's first college. It's now a nondescript car park but the building on the far (or eastern) side of this court still looks much as it did then, being the back of medieval university buildings. When King's started, it was the School of Canon Law, soon to be studied by several of the College's advanced Fellows. It also held part of the University Library behind the upper windows; scholars attempting to work in the library called out in Latin to the scholars of King's playing in the court below to cease disturbing them. The building on the left (or north) as you look in, now Caius library, is wider than the old King's buildings and the open space of the Old Court extended further in that direction, lapping round the corner of the canon law building.

Unfortunately, the other existing buildings on the first King's site do not take us far in appreciating the nature of the original college. After the University bought it from King's in 1829, they knocked down nearly all the King's buildings on the misplaced assumption that they needed the whole site for extending the University Library.

So all that physically remains of the original King's is the bottom half of the gatehouse; it's the bottom half because King's never managed to get it up to the roof and later engravings show the cut off stumps of the uncompleted turrets sprouting trees. Still, the entrance is the original entrance to King's College, resting on the (unfound) foundation stone set in person by the Founder, and the windows above the arch are also original. The demolished accommodation was in traditional staircases, with Scholars sleeping four to a room and Fellows two to a room with initially unglazed windows and heat only available in the hall.

Cramped as this accommodation was, it was where King's lived, ate, and studied for the next several hundred years, apart from going to look at the building site thoughtfully provided by the Founder to the south. They could soon see some foundations there and indeed, after only seventy years, a new chapel to contemplate but had to wait nearly three hundred years before anyone got any more living space. However, right from the start they had two buildings in addition to those already described. King Henry's officers in preparation for the 1441 foundation had also bought two hostels south of the Trinity Hall garden on what is now the rather gloomy area of grass between the Chapel and the Old Schools. On this additional part of the original site was built the first King's College Chapel, which lasted nearly a hundred years and where, by the Statutes, attendance was required twice a day by all. The other building constructed in this first phase was the first Provost's Lodge. This was at the eastern end of the same strip of land, where the large chestnut tree now grows beside King's Parade. (In the eighteenth century this land was sold to the University on its misplaced assumption that it was needed to build a library.)

The fact that a special large building was built for the Provost fits with the Founder's Statutes, even though it was nowhere near the place specified in his 'Will'. It is the first major feature distinguishing King's from the previous run of small medieval colleges. In them, the Master was very like the Fellows, living among them and not being paid much more. From the start a different style was set in King's that only later became normal in other colleges, with the head having his own considerable house. Living grandly on the High Street, he was sometimes called 'the Provost of Cambridge'. The Statutes allowed him a gentleman in waiting, five other menservants, and a stable with ten horses charged to the College. His annual stipend of £100 was a tenth of the College's entire income and massively more than any other Cambridge head; it was the financially most desirable position in the University.

As we can see and now know, King's survived. But it could so easily have been a short, optimistic, experiment by a young king that perished in the realities of madness, war, deposition, and death. And at first after the Founder's deposition, it did indeed seem that this is what would happen. The new king, Edward IV, revoked all the grants of his deposed rival so that the College's income was reduced from a thousand pounds a year to zero. The College pawned its plate to create a legal fighting fund but the omens must have been against success. The College had been founded by a king of one party (the Lancastrians), which were now unfortunately the defeated party in a civil war. So why should the new victorious party (the Yorkists) bother? The new king did not immediately abolish the College, re-granting the land on which it stood, including the building site. But the supposedly secure call on the King's property that was meant for twenty years to provide the funds to build a chapel and new court simply disappeared. So the second King's, the new college of the Founder's Will, could not be built. The estates providing an income to meet living expenses were more of a mixed story. Initially, King Edward ordered the money to be paid to himself rather than to the College. But after a year and a bit he relented sufficiently to grant some of them again, such as the ones mentioned above. This still meant that the College's income was halved, forcing it to reduce its complement by two thirds. The Founder's Statutes ordained that there was to be a total of 70 Scholars and Fellows and this number had indeed been reached early in the 1450s. In 1465, after Edward had taken over, the 70 had been radically reduced to 23.

The survival and later gradual recovery was in part because the College and its members, then as often later, learnt to work with the realities of power. Founded by the Lancastrians, it now had to work with the Yorkists and so operated a mutually beneficial circle by which College members occasionally helped the Court and the Court in turn occasionally helped the College. Thomas Rotherham was a great power in church and state under the new regime; he was also one of the earliest members of the College. He entered in 1443, proceeded in normal fashion to a Fellowship in 1446, was Bursar in 1447, and Vice Provost in 1456. Then, after leaving the College, he was Secretary of State to Edward IV, Lord Chancellor, and Archbishop of York. Complete servant of the usurping Yorkists, he continued to give gifts to the College as well as leaving it a legacy; he was a useful friend at Court. Walter Field, who entered two years after Rotherham in 1445, went the other direction, from Court to King's, returning as Provost from 1479 to 1499. Chaplain to Edward IV, he was a King's man in King's, giving the College contact again with royal power. Further estates were transferred to the College, income was restored to three quarters of the original level, and, crucially, royal grants were again made specifically for building. King Edward visited the College, work resumed on the building site, and the College stood again with the Court as it had in good King Henry's days. The only thing Edward did not do was re-found the College, saving centuries of misplaced apostrophes.

Michael Palmer, who entered after Rotherham and Field in 1458, was an untypical undergraduate. He went to fight for the Founder and was killed in his cause at the Second Battle of St Albans. But more typical was another entrant in the same year, John Argentein. Instead of fighting and dying as an undergraduate, he progressed through the full extended course of study in the College, first Arts, then teaching undergraduates as an MA, then studying theology and being ordained before starting his medical studies, taught by another Fellow of the College. He went to Ferrara to complete his medical education (and always inscribed his books in

Italian). Doctor of Medicine and Theology, trained and serviceable to kings, he used these accomplishments to play with power. He became a physician to the court, starting with the Yorkist court of Edward IV but continuing happily through the regime changes as royal physician; families come and go and kings kill each other but they all equally wanted good doctors with the sort of advanced science that could be provided by Cambridge (and Italy). Argentein, as their physician, was the last recorded person to see alive the princes who disappeared, presumed murdered, in the Tower of London after King Edward's death in 1483.

Under Henry VII, Argentein returned to King's as Provost; he had helped the power of the Court and the Court now helped him to power. An earlier example of such playing with existing power and returning to the College as its Provost is John Dogget. He came in 1451, was a Fellow in the later 1450's, and this time took the legal route after the divinity studies that led to his DD. Like Argentein, he went to Italy, becoming an LL.D. of Bologna. After that, he happily worked for the Yorkists as ambassador to both the Pope and the King of Denmark before returning to King's as Provost. The Provost in fact that had the hardest time was the one who stayed in King's and did not in the same way come from the Court with Court contacts and access to royal power. This was Robert Wodelarke, who was Provost when Argentein and Dogget were Students and Fellows, and who had to try and save the College in the initial grim times after the Founder's deposition; he was Provost from 1452 to 1479. Wodelarke did his best and used some of his own money, but with royal supply cut off there was no way that he could keep the building going. Intriguingly, he did find the time and money to start St Catharine's College next door and for the first two years of its existence combined being Master of Catz with being Provost of King's before inserting Richard Roche (who had already been 25 years a Fellow of King's) as its first independent Master. Given the syllabus that Wodelarke devised for St Catharine's, it has been speculated that he thought the King's ethos too utilitarian (with all those trained people emerging as doctors or lawyers) and wanted a college of more purely theological speculation. Alternatively, it could be that he prepared a lifeboat against the eventuality of his main ship capsizing, holed as it was below the waterline by lack of funds.

After the Founder's heir had been defeated and killed at the Battle of Tewkesbury on 4 May 1471, Edward IV had no longer any need to keep his father alive and had an opportunity to extinguish the entire line. So on 21 May 1471, as soon as he returned to London after the battle, he had Henry killed where he was held captive in the Tower. Every year on the exact anniversary of the day of his death and where a brass plate optimistically says is the exact spot where he was killed, the Provost of Eton and the Provost of King's lay lilies and roses, the respective emblems of their foundations, in memory of their joint murdered founder. The room in the Wakefield Tower is very likely where it happened. Because he was a royal saint, it was naturally supposed that he must have been killed saying his prayers and so the plate marking the spot is in a tiny oratory off the main room, into which the two provosts have to squeeze in turn to lay their floral tributes. Above this passing show, the oratory's stained glass window has a more permanent record, showing shields with the three white roses of King's and the three white lilies of Eton.

The battles and regime changes just described were part of what we call the Wars of the Roses (which, unsurprisingly, was somewhat more complicated than might here appear). In this context, people are sometimes puzzled by the whiteness of these roses, thinking that a Lancastrian foundation should have the red rose of Lancaster rather than the white rose of York. But King's was founded well before the war and got its current arms with three white roses in 1449, when the King was uniquely king and had no need to indicate a side in a disputed inheritance. What Henry wanted was white for purity for his two colleges dedicated to Our Lady, the spotless blessed virgin. The supposed incident in the Temple Garden of picking roses, represented in Shakespeare's *Henry VI*, was later and even then, when sides were formed and war started, tying them up with roses is something of a later conceit (as when Shakespeare was writing, or the chronicles from which he drew). There are roses all over the Chapel, both carved in stone in the antechapel and in the glass. But this is all after the end of the wars, when the first Tudor king, Henry VII, wished to make the point that he had blended the roses, being Lancastrian by inheritance and Yorkist by marriage. His Tudor rose is of both colours and is displayed in the windows as well as pure reds and pure whites; we have to imagine that if the large stiff stone roses in the antechapel were coloured, they would be mixed roses with both red and white petals.

Having examined the royal saint's what and how, I end with the why. Why did Henry do it? What was he trying to achieve? And why did he choose Cambridge rather than Oxford, then a much larger, more prestigious and successful university? After all, Oxford is in the centre of England whereas it has always been a puzzle (at least to Oxford historians) how a university ever came into being at the edge of the eastern miasmic fens. The King was copying Wykeham's great plan; Wykeham had paired his school with Oxford; and Oxford is just up the river from Eton and easily accessible.

Part of the answer lies in the King's advisers, who contained several Cambridge men with a natural preference for their own university (just as Wykeham, an Oxford man, had for his). Henry had been guided by them in how he framed his first plan and when it all became bigger and more serious, it may have seemed simpler to extend the previous plan than start all over again and buy up the centre of Oxford. (Otherwise we'd have had St Nicholas' College in Cambridge, King's College in Oxford, and I wouldn't be writing this.) One thing that the Founder was supposed to have said, and which has been rejected as a myth by earnest Cambridge figures since the seventeenth century, was that he felt that he had to do something for Cambridge in an attempt to raise it nearer the level of Oxford.

The best single answer is none of the above and gets back to the main question of what Henry was trying to achieve. A leading factor for Henry and his advisers in choosing Cambridge was that, unlike Oxford, it was not tainted with heresy. It may be ironical in view of the later history of King's, and indeed of Cambridge, but the College was founded where it was to make it orthodox. Oxford had recently produced in Wycliffe someone who seemed to be a heretic to more than his dialectical opponents and the Founder's Statutes end with a declaration to be made by all Kingsmen that they forswear Wycliffe. In the Provost's Lodge at King's there is an ancient and gloomy picture of Wycliffe of uncertain provenance. Given that King's was founded specifically to combat Wycliffe and all his works, when I was living there I wondered why the College had acquired the enemy's picture but fantasised that it worked like a police mug shot, warning everyone what to avoid. Beside it currently hangs the beguiling mistress of the man who murdered the Founder, posing a more naked question about the College's choice of its visual representation of its founding times.

Henry's aim was to produce a highly educated clergy for use in Church and State, with the supposed side benefit of putting down heresy. His plan is specifically stated in the preamble to his Statutes. He founds his college, as it may be translated into English, "to uphold and exalt the Christian faith, to further the Holy Church, and to extend the liberal arts and departments of learning and skill." The four statutory objects of the current college, as first stated in the nineteenth century and embraced in the 1923 Oxford & Cambridge Act, are that it is a place of Education, Religion, Learning, and Research. With due adjustment for language, this is already in the Founder's statement. Religion is clearly there but so also, importantly, is Education. Learning (*scienciae*) is specifically mentioned but so also is the idea of extension (*augmentum*) of knowledge, or what we later call Research. Conspicuously a place of religion, it was important for King Henry that he wasn't just founding a chapel but instead a college devoted to the advancement and transmission of learning.

With a mixture of ages and levels of intellectual authority, it was to form a single intellectual community, bound by the same ends, the same founder and the same formative experience, having all been to the same school.

In this chapter, we have seen how King's started as another college like the others, hidden away, for senior academics, and sitting on a relatively modest footprint. We have also seen how, at least in plan, it transmuted into something much bigger in its numbers and the amount of the town that it arrogated to itself for its sole collegiate purpose. This created an anomaly, a most unusual college. Some aspects of the anomaly provided a precedent, setting a standard that was matched and exceeded by later entrants. But some, such as a sister school, stayed anomalous, making King's special until relatively recently. Among the copied aspects is the idea of a royal and rich college, dominating all the land between the High Street and the river. After the foundation of King's, in turn Queens', St John's, and Trinity aimed at this and the baton of being the premier college passed down the Backs (or, indeed, created the Backs).

The founding royal saint, and hence his saintly foundation, had big ideas. But so far in this story, they remain only ideas. The actual college on the ground has a modest court in a back street and has only recently just managed to squeak into survival. As compared with what we later know, it is a college in a different place, with a different chapel, and speaking a different language. It has a monastic life, male, unmarried, and with daily prayer. Clearly a considerable story remains to be told.

CHAPTER TWO

THE KINGS' CHAPEL

B uilding requires both will and means, and while the infant College had the will it only infrequently had the means. The story of built King's is therefore a story of when the College was given the money; similarly, the story of unbuilt King's is of when it failed to find it. As we saw, the Founder planned a supply of money to complete his college. Then, as we also saw, he was defeated, deposed, and the additional money needed for building disappeared, leaving an unbuilt great court and a project for a great chapel.

This chapter describes how, in contrast to the court, the chapel was indeed built with the magnificent size and quality of the Founder's extravagant plan. The unbuilt accommodation, hall, and library need no explanation beyond the disappearance of the means required to fund them. But the planned chapel was also unbuilt at this point; less than a tenth of its walls and roof had been constructed. Nevertheless, unlike the other buildings, it got completed so that the College ended up with the Founder's chapel although it never achieved the Founder's court. It is therefore an especially significant building in terms of the College's embodied memory. To touch the Chapel today is to make physical content with the foundation, linking present to the far distant past. Hearing its choir sing there today is to participate in a tradition that recognisably reaches back to this alien period. The Chapel is by a long way the College's best known building; it is its aesthetically most significant one; and it is also the oldest building that is still used by the College. It embodies half a millennium of College history and, as the first realisation of the Founder's sacred plan, it forms a fitting next step in our story. It started; it stopped; it started again; it stopped again; but somehow it got completed.

Started by a king, its continuation was only achieved by other kings. The chief ones are all usefully called 'Henry' and they, unsurprisingly, contributed in numerical order: Henry VI, Henry VII, and Henry VIII. (The College is still waiting for Henry IX; after King Henry VIII, there have been no further kingly contributions to King's.) Two other kings were also involved: Edward IV and Richard III. The general picture is of shorter phases of activity interspersed with longer interludes of inaction. Each battle-forced change in the ruling dynasty froze activity and by the time usurpers had been thawed out they in turn were at risk of being replaced.

Even before the start of the civil war and the Founder's deposition, he had been in trouble. France was being lost (Joan of Arc) and the peasants were revolting (Jack Cade). (The much quoted Shakespearean line, "let's kill all the lawyers" is said by a follower of Cade; lawyers were, as we saw, part of the product of the King's college in Cambridge.) Yet good initial progress was made with the Founder's plan. A master mason responsible for the great abbey at Bury St Edmunds, Reginald Ely, was appointed. His competence can still be seen in the original gatehouse and in the 1440s he also completed the first chapel. The Founder arranged an enlarged supply of money for his enlarged college and a supply of good building stone from Yorkshire. Down the Wharfe and Humber and up the Ouse and Cam, this arrived at the newly cleared riverside and Reginald Ely used it to lay the foundations of the second enormous chapel, exactly on the dimensions listed in the Founder's 'Will'. This was for a church of overall 288 foot length, divided into two parts by a central 14 foot wide screen.

Any architect would have had to make some additions or adjustments to the Founder's detailed plan as it failed to mention doors and so provide any way of getting in or out of the edifice. It looks as if Reginald Ely may have planned these for the middle of the sides, entering under the organ screen. He built all the walls up to about six feet in height and in the same way started the base of the accommodation on the east side of the great court. This ran along the line of the present King's Parade screen, with chambers being served by spiral staircases in external towers (as is the case with the Chapel). At the Chapel's east end, the building was taken part way up the great windows and until the nineteenth century the lower half of the most south east window was of stone instead of glass because it was assumed that it would be an internal wall between the Chapel and the connected court accommodation.

However, this never happened. The accommodation never got that high and its base can be seen in later engravings, still stretching south and waiting to be completed. The Chapel building similarly stopped. A good idea of how far it had reached can be seen by looking across the Front Court and tracing out the white and the yellower stone; Ely had built in white and when they started again, the stone colour changes. Similarly on the north side, the progress and pause can be traced in the white stone, high up the windows at the east end and then descending to near ground level as it moves west. We have an unusable rump, a romantic ruin. As described in the last chapter, Provost Wodelarke desperately tried to keep building going. He could find the funding to found another college but he couldn't touch anything this scale. He made an appeal to the Fellowship. This raised £10.97 (in modern decimal notation; £10-19-4 in old money). Clearly that wasn't going to take it far; the total cost of the fabric alone came to about £15,000 and little over £1,000 had been spent by this stage. So a massive amount of funding had still to be found.

This was partly because of the lavish specification in the Founder's 'Will'. He wanted the Chapel vaulted (that is, with a stone ceiling under its pitched timber and leaded roof). Yet it was only cathedrals that were vaulted, not private college chapels. Henry was copying William of Wykeham's foundation in Oxford with a large court and large chapel (although Henry made sure that his were larger). But New College Chapel is not vaulted, nor is All Souls in Oxford, another college founded before King's with an intended impressive chapel. A hundred years later, King Henry VIII founded a royal college in the centre of Cambridge. It was magnificent; it was well endowed; it was a grand royal enterprise with a large stone built chapel. But even this dazzling display of royal power did not have a stone vault.

So both in its size and its nature, this was a very expensive operation. It also lacked an obvious point. It was the second of the King's planned chapels, called in the College accounts the 'new church' or the 'new temple'; the College already had a working chapel, adequate for its needs. The citizens of Cambridge, contemplating their removed houses, saw them replaced by not one, not two, but three churches in construction; they might have wondered about what their king was doing. (It's three because a church had to be knocked down to build the second chapel and the Founder insisted that it be rebuilt, which it was on the north side of the Old Court.) Massively expensive, with no immediate point, and with its mad supporter deprived and disappeared, all attempts at the Chapel's completion inevitably imposed almost insoluble problems. Consider what would happen today if most of the Chapel was removed by some disaster, leaving only the base of its walls and a fragment at the east end. After such a cataclysm, there would be a natural desire to rebuild and restore the Founder's great project. Yet even if the current College spent every bit of its endowment, so that it would not be able to do anything else ever again, it would still not have enough to restore its chapel; in fact the current College cannot even afford to insure it against this eventuality. So it would have to appeal to others, hoping to interest either a very rich private benefactor or else the state on the supposition that it was an important national monument.

Here we reach the point of kings. For in the fifteenth century, kings were both; that is, they were both great private landholders and also personal rulers of what we now call the state.

So if King's was to be saved, it would have to be done by kings. We saw in the last chapter how Court contacts counted and how it was only when the new king, Edward IV, installed his chaplain as Provost of King's that the money again started to flow. In all, King Edward provided something over a thousand pounds, which was the amount that the Founder had planned annually for twenty years to complete his college. A new master mason, Simon Clerk, was appointed. Unfortunately, King Edward died only three years after his conversion to aiding the College. But luckily his successor, Richard III, took on and indeed increased the momentum, pushing in £700 and specifically ordering more rapid progress. The new master mason managed to complete the walls of the eastern five bays and even, it would seem, install a timber roof above them.

And then, again, disaster. King Richard might have been vigorous about the Chapel. But he had also been vigorous in other directions (such as murdering Edward IV's heirs in the Tower). So there was sufficient disaffection to enable the prospect of a successful rebellion by Henry of Monmouth, head of the Lancastrians. He made a pact with disaffected Yorkists, left France, invaded, gathered forces, marched to battle, and defeated and killed King Richard. He consequentially took on the country (as King Henry VII). But even though a Lancastrian like the Founder, he did not take on King's. Everything stopped again and the College was returned to its old problem, still with the great majority of the money to find and left to moulder through another twenty year hiatus caused by regime change.

It could easily have stopped at this point with an unusable and unrequired peculiar rump of a grand project, as high as it was long. A good comparison is Eton Chapel. The Founder wanted his two colleges to have the same kind of chapels, laying out matching dimensions for each and with both vaulted. At this point, similarly halted, Eton decided that they had no option other than to scrap their vault and their planned western half. Its sister Cambridge college could very easily have done the same thing at the same time for the same reasons and some building details from that time show that this was probably planned. Yet, although Eton never completed its chapel, we with hindsight know that King's did. Somehow, surprisingly, the puzzle was subsequently solved.

Chapel is both building and use and nobody could be persuaded to complete the building unless they saw the point of its use. So also for us: before seeing the solution we should first understand its intended use. It was always meant to be more than a large religious space and, copying New College Oxford, King's was more monastic in its style than most colleges. So as well as a daily mass, there were to be frequent services every day (corresponding to the monastic offices). In addition, and importantly, the chapel services were not just for the living members of the community but also for the dead. It was a time when people were particularly concerned with their passage through purgatory after they died and before they reached paradise. The prayers of the living were thought to be an important aid in this process and so people built chapels, called chantry chapels, and endowed clergy to serve them by saying frequent masses for their souls after they died as well as for the souls of their already dead relatives. Common at this period, it was also part of the specific point of King's College Chapel as planned by the Founder and described in his Statutes. Masses were to be said for him after his death and also for his father and mother. Other individuals giving money to the College similarly specified in return an annual posthumous mass for their soul. Provosts created what were in effect chantry chapels, where they planned their burial; Provost Argentein, whom we met in the last chapter, so arranged the most south eastern side chapel.

Services require people to celebrate mass, to say the offices, to pray for the souls of the dead, and to sing. Even though much, such as the psalms, would be in plainsong, more expert singing was required for the daily antiphon and for special services. In the Founder's Statutes, the College is required to employ ten priests, who were known as conducts, to service the Chapel. South of the old Provost's Lodge (and so on what is now the grass outside the screen and to the right as you enter the front gate) was Conducts' Court, which was where they lived. So although many Fellows were priests and both Fellows and Scholars would be familiar with singing services, the College was given by the Founder an additional specially employed cadre of clergy to maintain the Chapel's work. If and when it was finished, ten altars were planned so that each conduct could have his own altar at which he could say his daily private mass and dedicate it, as required, to the care of the dead. But this posse of priests, living in their priestly colony beside the rest of the college, did not wait for the possible completion of the Chapel. We saw in the last chapter how the numbers of Scholars and Fellows planned by the Founder for his new enlarged college soon reached the seventy specified in the Statutes, even though there was nowhere beyond the original court for them to live. So also the salaried clergy soon reached the specified ten, even though there was nowhere beyond the first chapel for them to sing and pray.

This applies also to another important part of the chapel provision, the choristers. Sixteen choristers were specified in the Founder's Statutes to sing the high parts. Furthermore, great care was taken to make sure that the College had the best voices. Repeated commissions were given by kings to press choristers from elsewhere. So an ambitious choirmaster could scour the country, finding good boys' voices in Fotheringhay (or London, or Windsor, or Oxford) so that he could seize them (like a later naval press gang) and force them to come and live near the conducts and sing in a chapel in Cambridge while they were being given a grammar school education. (Like rival football teams, the pressing sometimes came the other way, so that other royal choirs could occasionally forcibly poach, on royal authority, promising voices from King's.) The choristers' status varied, so that at some times they had the role of serving food in hall but sometimes had their own table. The hall in medieval King's was like the hall of a medieval manor house with everyone eating dinner together in their own appropriate places, including the conducts, choristers, and other employees. And singing wasn't just in chapel; they sang together religiously in hall at the end of the meal as well as carols and more secular songs on special occasions.

It will be remembered how the Founder re-founded King's to make it a single project with his other college at Eton. In his Statutes for Eton, choristers from his Cambridge college were given special preference in selection. The choristers were taken annually to Eton to be assessed and at least 13 were selected during this period, most of whom returned to become Scholars and Fellows at King's. Robert Ambrose and Brian Esthorpe, for example, were choristers together in the 1460s who both returned as Scholars in 1471 before becoming Fellows. John St George was a chorister who came back to the College as a Scholar in 1476. After a short period as a Fellow, he left in 1483 to go into Mount Grace, the Carthusian monastery in Yorkshire; all that quasi-monastic singing was insufficient and, like others in this early period, he left the Fellowship to join a real monastery.

This rich religious life all unfolded in the original small chapel. Due care was taken of the dead and so sang the living. Adequate for the College's needs, it sharpens to the question of whether anything might or should be made of the Founder's folly beside it. Another chapel was not required, or if it was, the stump of the project might be made fit for use. The good stone could have been carried away to help in the construction of other colleges. But in fact, as we know, it was finished. There might have been hope with Henry VII defeating wicked King Richard and taking over the kingdom; after all, the Founder's side, the Lancastrians, were back again in power. Later, when the new king installed the royal physician as Provost, there might again have been hope. Argentein wrote to the King reminding him of his uncle's uncompleted project. Yet nothing; nothing happened; and the folly remained.

To understand how the ice eventually broke we need again to identify people who counted at Court. The first decisive person was someone as far inside its centre as it was possible to be, the

King's mother, Lady Margaret Beaufort. She had given birth to Henry VII when only thirteen, so she was nearer him in age than being his mother might imply. She was rich in her own right and shrewd; she was closely of the family; and she was a central broker in the conspiracy with dissident Yorkists that had brought him to the throne. Trusted by the King, her backing of a project would inevitably be influential. Lady Margaret was by this stage widowed, living a pious life in her own right and dependent on her confessor and chaplain, John Fisher. Here we take the trail back to Cambridge. Fisher, Bishop of Rochester, was Chancellor of the University and, through Lady Margaret's influence, the President of Queens' College; he was also the first Lady Margaret Professor of Divinity. In his care for the University as its Chancellor, Fisher identified several projects in which he managed to interest Lady Margaret. There was getting the translated Godshouse restarted as an important college: Lady Margaret endowed it and re-founded it as Christ's College. There was making something of the decayed Hospital of St John near the Jewry: Lady Margaret died before the money could be transferred but through Fisher's heroic efforts, it got posthumously founded as St John's College by use of her legacy. And then there was the matter of the royal saint's uncompleted chapel, an unpleasant question mark brooding over Cambridge for anyone looking out the back of the President's Lodging at Queens'.

Or for their guests. What did the trick were two visits to Cambridge made by King Henry VII towards the end of his life and reign. The first was in April 1507, when he came with his mother, devout patron of Cambridge causes. Naturally they stayed in Queens' as Fisher's guests. They had come for the annual St George's Day celebration of the premier order of chivalry, the Knights of the Garter, which could not be held in its normal place at St George's Chapel in Windsor because of refurbishment. The service was instead held in the Founder's first chapel, next door at King's; already richly furnished, it was specially got up with stall decorations for the Knights of the Garter. Reaching it from Queens' meant passing the rump of the King's uncle's grand project and Fisher (and no doubt also Lady Margaret) managed to have a word in the King's ear. In response, the King gave a little money to make new contracts for the Chapel's completion.

Next year the royal party returned, the King, the King's Mother, and also this time the prince who later became Henry VIII. Again, they stayed in Queens'. Again, they would have been very conscious of the rump of the King's uncle's grand project. This time they attended the University's annual degree ceremony and Fisher made a speech, cleverly thanking the King for his great support for Cambridge. Only a king he said, correctly, could complete King's College Chapel. More money came from the King and the King's Mother was firmly in support; it would not only be a royal but also a family project, fittingly celebrating the Lancastrian Saint as well as the king who had personally supervised the betrothal of Lady Margaret with the King's father, Edmund Tudor.

King Henry VII has had a reputation for meanness. It was more that he was careful with money and knew and checked exactly how it was spent. In this he was very different from the Founder, who was generous to a fault, not interested in adding up, and indeed even had to pawn goods to find ready money for his marriage. But King Henry VII was willing to spend when he was convinced of the importance of a project. And among his projects were to produce fitting memorials of his uncle, the royal saint. One such was to have him formally canonised by the Vatican. In this he failed, perhaps because he did not spend enough money on it in bribes but more probably because the Vatican did not wish to canonise someone thought to be half mad. (This was not the later, more spiritual, Vatican ready to canonise holy fools.) Yet King Henry was clearly a people's saint, even if the Vatican was unpersuaded. He posthumously performed miracles; he was extensively invoked; and he was a natural object of pilgrimage. One of Henry VII's major projects was to extend Westminster Abbey to provide the suitable pilgrimage site by reburying Henry VI there. (In the event this extension east was used for his own burial.)

Cambridge was out of the way, it was not London, and it would not be a pilgrimage site. Nevertheless, completing his great chapel formed a natural part of a commemorative plan for the royal saint.

Once convinced, King Henry VII acted. In 1509 he provided as careful a plan as his uncle, not now concerned with the architectural details but with the proper flow of money, both in his own life (which he knew would not be long) and also after his death. Furthermore, unlike his uncle, his careful financial plan worked and was sufficient to complete the building. The King paid an immediate £5000 and ordered that a firm chest be found to put it in, with four locks and four keys. This was to be kept in the College's Treasury (which was the room above the arch in the old gateway whose windows still exist). The Provost, the Bursar, the Vice Chancellor, and the man who paid the workmen all had keys and they, or their representatives, had to be all present together to extract any money. Three weeks later the King was dead but the carefully drawn document protected the continued flow of funds with a second tranche of another £5000 provided in 1512.

Argentein was still Provost during the first visit and the King had come to dine with his old physician in King's. But by the time the money was placed in the College Treasury there was another Provost holding the key, Robert Hacumblen. Hacumblen oversaw the agreements for the different parts of the building work and, with both accounts and contracts surviving from this period, we know in detail how it was undertaken. The new master mason employed was John Wastell and starting the work had to wait until he had completed the fan vault of the tower crossing at Canterbury Cathedral. Once arrived, he raised the walls at the west end and vaulted with the largest fan vault ever built the complete length of the Chapel. He built the battlements and their pinnacles as well as the four corner towers. (One was built first as a trial and when Hacumblen acting for the College deemed it to be satisfactory, he was given the contract for the three others.) He fan-vaulted the side chapels, apart from the already vaulted north easterly ones, and the whole building was completed in 1515.

It has already been seen from the kind of stone how the Chapel was built not just from bottom to top but also from east to west. The Founder in his 'Will' wanted it to be sparse in decoration. ("I will that the edification of my same college proceed in large form, clear and substantial, setting aside superfluity of too great curious works of entaille and busy moulding.") This was not, at the top and west end, how it actually emerged once the new dynasty was in charge. Looking across the Front Court, it is easy to see where the buttresses change and start to be decorated. Inside, the antechapel is a riot of busy stone moulding in comparison with the more sombre eastern half. It shouts its status as a family project in which Henry VII commemorates not only his royal uncle but also himself and his family come again to the throne. The two most common stone symbols are a crowned portcullis and a crowned rose. They alternate in the great central bosses in the fan vault; they sit equally at the tops of the corner towers; they alternate externally on the more western buttresses and the internal decoration of the west wall. They are crowned to show that they are royal symbols. We already met with the large stiff rose in the last chapter as the symbol of the union of the former two warring parties by blending the red rose of Lancaster with the white rose of York. This is the Tudor rose; King Henry VII's statement of what he and his wife had achieved. (The later windows are less impartial, having 94 red roses to 13 blended roses; basically, the Lancastrians had won.) The portcullis, the gate of a fort, symbolises Beaufort, the family name of the King's Mother. Over every door of the side chapels are Henry VII's royal arms supported by a dragon on the left and a greyhound on the right. The Tudors were a Welch family; hence the dragon (which would be red if coloured) and the greyhound was an old Lancastrian emblem that was specially granted to Henry VII's Welsh father.

Once the walls, vault, and roof were completed, the Chapel still had to be glazed and furnished. This also took longer than anticipated, so that the second chapel was not yet quite ready for use when the first chapel suddenly fell down in 1537. In all, it took a hundred years from conception and the world in which it was finally completed was a different world from the world in which it was conceived. The furnishing, flooring, and glazing were funded by Henry VIII, to whom Hacumblen now had to write his begging letters. However, the new king kept supporting it, and he had also made no attempt to disturb his father's settlement for completing the fabric when he first came to the throne. This new world of Henry VIII is described in the next chapter; I complete this present one on the Chapel by dissecting a small part of it as it exists today.

For this I select the second side chapel on the right after entry. It is open to visitors and the first thing that the visitor notices is the modern bossy college protecting itself against visitors with roped off areas and notices to keep out. It is a stately home on display; thou shalt not touch. The next thing noticed is a massive marble tomb that fills most of the space, chilly cold and sharply contrasting in its classical style with the surrounding architecture. It is here that the Chapel most resembles the jumble of inserted monuments and tombs in cathedrals or Westminster Abbey. There are monuments on the eastern wall and the whole of the western one is filled with a colourful tribute to Samuel Collins, Regius Professor of Divinity, Provost of the College, deprived in the English Civil War. Leaning against the far wall is an ancient crane, reminding of the building and adding to the side chapel's feeling of being a disorganised box of curiosities.

The tomb is of the only son and presumptive heir of the great first Duke of Marlborough, dead shortly before his father embarked on his dazzling series of victories that brought the sun king Louis XIV back to earth. Student at King's, the heir died in College while still an undergraduate. (The body started underneath the tomb but was later repatriated to Blenheim Palace, the family seat.) We might try to squeeze past the far, permitted, side to try and read the inscription on the back, only to be stopped by a pile of chairs, reminding us that these side chapels tend to get used as dumping grounds and that the antechapel, now and from its start, has also been used for secular purposes. Or perhaps it might be a harpsichord, waiting like the chairs for an antechapel concert. If we do manage to see the far side of the tomb, we find a long Latin description of the unfortunate Marquess by his College Tutor, Francis Hare. Already notable at Eton, Hare was a leading Latinist and taught his tutorial pupils a refined and critical taste. Among them was Robert Walpole, later long term prime minister and presenter to bishoprics; Hare ended up as Bishop of Chichester and might well have been Archbishop of Canterbury. Earlier, through the Marlborough contact, he was Chaplain-General to the Duke's forces during the famous victories which Hare described in his letters; he was still a Fellow while abroad with the army.

This much is the added accumulation of centuries; we can now search beneath, behind, and above the debris, seeking the Chapel as it was first constructed. The glass between the side chapel and the antechapel is original. Able to get much closer to it than that in the great windows, we can examine early sixteenth century glass, admire its shimmer and the gently distorted vision it gives of the antechapel. The saints at the top are also original, from the Chapel's catholic, pre-Reformation, medieval purpose. They are St Christopher and St Ursula on the left, St Anne and John the Baptist on the right. In between is the Annunciation: on the left the Angel Gabriel hailing Mary (with the Latin speech bubble coming from his mouth, saying hail, full of grace) and the Blessed Virgin herself responding on the right (saying, in her Latin bubble, behold the handmaid of the Lord). St Mary is one of the two saints to whom the College is dedicated and the Founder's Statutes required a sermon each year in the Chapel on the feast day being displayed here. This day (Lady Day, March 25th) was then the first day of the year and for its first three hundred years the College therefore thought that it was founded in 1440, the same year as its sister college at Eton (rather than as we now think 1441, the year after Eton). It is amazing that this easily accessible representation of the Annunciation to Mary survived later iconoclasm; the eighteenth century antiquarian William Cole reports it as being painted over, so this is perhaps the explanation.

The outer glass looking to the Court is mainly nineteenth century replacement but the half figures in the middle are original. Here we have the Founder and St Nicholas, his patron saint. Observing his pious gaze and his twin crowns, this is as near the Founder as we are likely to get. St Nicholas (Santa Claus), the other saint to whom the College is dedicated, reminds us of the long College connection with Christmas. That is, if this is St Nicholas; traditionally identified as such in old accounts of the Chapel, it may be merely a myth and it may also be that St Nicholas was once here and has now disappeared.

Having captured the glass and the Founder, if not perhaps Santa Claus, we now look up at the ceiling. Here, again, we are much nearer than normal a famous aspect of the Chapel. We have a fan vault, just above our heads, close up, ready for inspection. But as we do, the first startling thing that we see is that it is partly painted. Used as we are to the chilly purity of the ruins of classical temples, noble, nude, and antique, it is a shock to discover that the temples in use were probably brightly painted. So also here with the Chapel. Used to the serene, pale, unruffled procession of the enormous fan vault, it is startling to realise that it too might all have been brightly painted. Provost Hacumblen, writing to King Henry about what was needed for completion of the Chapel, listed "the gilding and painting of the great vault." Prior to the Reformation stripping of the English altars, this is how churches were and just because the Chapel windows provide a coloured story would not have inhibited further bright colour on the ceiling.

Finally we return to the fenced off part, which might (if only because it was prohibited) have first attracted our attention on entry. Here there is a wooden seat, a pew, making it like a church. As indeed it was; it had an altar on the opposite east end and this was a place for services. It was a place to say mass. It was a place to be used daily by one of the large bevy of ten employed priests provided by the Founder in his Statutes to tend the chapel. And it was more than just another altar, which a conduct would use daily for his private service. It was a chantry chapel. It is the resting place of Provost Hacumblen, whose (mutilated) brass still graces its floor and whose bones lie directly beneath our feet. He had it decorated in the 1520s, just before he died, with saints, painted vault, and his initials in the original shimmering glass between it and the antechapel. The floor brass pictures him like a medieval cleric and invokes our prayers; here prayers were to be said constantly, medieval fashion, speeding his soul through purgatory and on eventually to paradise. So we are standing on the man who signed the contracts for completion, installed the fan vaulting, and started commissioning the glass in the main chapel. The Bible read there at services leans against his prominently engraved name on the lectern he donated. Hacumblen was also a musician, a composer, and a strong supporter of the Choir. Here in the presence of his death are woven the three central strands of the Chapel: religion, architecture, and music.

CHAPTER THREE

ROYAL REFORMATIONS

We have seen how the infant college, founded by a king and dependent on kings, was diminished by conflict between kings and languished when it got out of contact with the ruling court. In the sixteenth century the problem changes from keeping in with competing royal dynasties to keeping in with competing royal religions. There was now a single dynasty in control throughout this century, known to us as the Tudors. But each of the five Tudor monarchs had a different religion and it was a period when the religion of the monarch was expected to be also the religion of the country. A college like King's, which supplied the state with officials and priests, had to conform and whatever was the correct royal religion of the day had not only to be publicly expressed in its chapel but also upheld by all its members who worshipped there together.

Royal power founded King's College to extirpate heresy. Forty years earlier, it enacted that heretics should be burnt, a more direct and cheaper method. There was, perhaps, at the time a touch of heresy in Oxford. But this did not trouble fifteenth century Cambridge; all the Fellows of King's swore an oath against heresy and that was that. However with the new century, a change in the monarch meant a change in what was considered heresy and failure to keep up with the Court could result in a much worse fate than the previous century's uncompleted court. When Oxford started scorching the front door of Balliol by burning heretics, the men they burnt were Cambridge graduates.

We left Provost Hacumblen in his chantry after planning the Chapel as its saintly Founder would have wished and looking in his brass effigy like an abbot who had rebuilt his medieval monastery. Yet within a few years, no monasteries are left in England; no chantry chapels; no shrines; no pilgrimages; no prayers for the souls of the faithful departed; and no more magic mystery in the mass. The high altar, centre point for the elaborate sung services, was erected in 1544 and the Catholic Chapel was finally furnished as its Catholic Founder would have wished. Five years later, the altar was taken apart and removed. So a hundred years of building gave a mere five years of use and before the Chapel was fully finished it had already forgone its founding function.

The insertion of the great stained glass windows in the Chapel was started by Hacumblen. Yet after his death, the story they depict changes to what can be directly sourced from the Bible rather than being taken from the accumulated tradition of the Catholic Church. Finally, when the College reached the great west window, it gave up and left it as clear glass. The natural medieval subject for this west window was the last judgement, matching the crucifixion at the east end. Yet in this changed religious world, visualising the last judgement was a step too far where there was no Biblical authority for the appearance of hell and purgatory, although there was a rich artistic tradition on which to draw. The west window stayed clear glass for centuries, upsetting the balance of its coloured companions. It was only stained in the nineteenth century (upsetting the balance in the other direction by making it too dark and detailed).

It is a century of rebirth, renewal, and reform with its two central movements being known as the Renaissance and the Reformation. The Chapel, structurally a late flowering of medieval gothic, gets clothed in the new classical Renaissance style; most obviously in the woodwork of the central screen. Similarly in learning, there is a new desire to reach behind the Latinate medieval culture for fresh and direct contact with its original classical sources. The seven year study in the Arts practised by students mainly derived from the Greek philosopher and scientist, Aristotle, considered in Latin texts and encrusted by medieval commentators. In the Renaissance, scholars went directly back to the original Greek texts and so produced a new learning. By the 1520s when Robert Hacumblen was in the Provost's Lodge planning his chantry chapel, John Bryan was in the College hall teaching the Scholars directly from the Greek text of Aristotle and without the intervening Latin commentators.

Central to a religious foundation training priests was the sacred book of its religion, the Bible; we saw in the first chapter how it was read daily in Latin in chapel and hall. Yet the Bible was not originally written in Latin but in Greek and Hebrew. Renaissance rebirth led back to it also being studied in its original languages with both Greek and Hebrew being taught in the College. The University Chancellor, John Fisher, was a strong promoter of this new learning. At the degree ceremony described in the last chapter, the degree of DD was awarded to Erasmus, the greatest scholar of this new Greek-based northern Renaissance. The idea was to lure Erasmus and the new learning to Cambridge. He did not come immediately, but when he came (in 1511) he connected with many at King's. John Bryan, who taught Greek in the hall, had been as an undergraduate one of his young friends and disciples. Richard Croke ('Crocus'), who entered King's in 1506, had been a pupil of Erasmus even before he came to Cambridge. Croke taught Greek in Louvain and Cologne and very successfully introduced it to Leipzig. He also was lured back to Cambridge by Chancellor Fisher to become the first Public Orator of the University.

Kings (such as Henry VII and Henry VIII) passed through Cambridge en route to the primary English place of pilgrimage, Walsingham. When Erasmus was in Cambridge he made a gently mocking visit to Walsingham, attended by another of his young King's disciples, Robert Aldrich. After Erasmus left Cambridge, he perfected his Greek Text of the New Testament, enabling the new scholars to read the Christian part of the Bible in its original language. One route from here (not taken by Erasmus himself) was to use this newly available Biblical text as evidence in questioning the official church doctrine that action in this life (such as purchasing indulgences, saying masses for the dead, or making pilgrimages to saints and holy places) could help souls after death. The Protestant Reformation is normally dated from Martin Luther nailing his theses against purchasing such a path through purgatory to a church door in Wittenberg in 1517. For these Protestants, salvation depended on faith rather than works and authority derived from the Bible rather than the Pope. So the Bible had to be translated into the vernacular; Luther translated it into German and his disciple Tyndale translated it into English.

A pub in King's Lane (now marked by a blue plaque on the College buildings in King's Parade) was a favourite meeting place to discuss the new ideas with an unobtrusive entrance for people from Queens' and King's. It was popularly known as 'Little Germany' because of its openness to Germanic reform and some of those open to reform in the 1520s were young Fellows of King's. When Cardinal Wolsey, the chief adviser to the King and chief power (after Henry) in the land, wanted to form a special new college called Cardinal's College in Oxford, he naturally dipped into King's to get the best scholars in the new learning to give his college a flying start. Unfortunately, the ones he drew out had been talking in Little Germany and so took the virus of Lutheranism to Oxford. One was imprisoned for his beliefs in the college cellars with nothing to eat but the stored salt beef; he died. Another (John Frith) got away and abroad, where he worked with Tyndale, but came back and wrote against the Catholic doctrine of transubstantiation; the young reformer was only thirty when burnt in the slow fire of Smithfield by Henry VIII for his beliefs. The most important was Richard Cox.

Fellow of King's in 1522 and teaching the new learning in Cardinal College in 1524, Headmaster of Eton while still in his twenties and later head of Wolsey's college, renamed Christ Church after Wolsey's disgrace, Cox was a great Protestant survivor whom we will encounter again.

In the sixteenth century, the University expanded from being basically a seminary for training priests (who might also, in the fashion of the time, take on important secular work) to become also a nursery for finishing the education of young gentlemen (before their important secular work). Correspondingly, the normal student ceased to be someone living in lodgings but became resident in a college that could look after him on behalf of his parents. These students, unsupported by college endowment, were called pensioners because they paid fees. Soon the normal college had many more pensioners than its supported scholars. King's similarly added fee paying students, although to a lesser extent than other colleges. In addition to the Scholars from Eton supported by the Founder's endowment, there were now Fellow Commoners and Scholar Commoners who paid different levels of fees as well as Sizars who worked their way through college. Their numbers stayed small, partly because these were unattractive positions at King's where only Scholars could become Fellows. Another reason was that without its planned court the College was seriously short of accommodation; later in the century, these additional students took over the rooms vacated by the no longer needed posse of Chapel priests but their numbers were at the same point explicitly limited to twelve.

We have seen how the training in canon law particularly helped with those becoming bishops, state servants, or acting as ambassadors. The new learning added a common European wide polish to the educated elite as they negotiated with similarly trained clerics in other countries. The young man going to Walsingham with Erasmus ended up as Bishop of Carlisle. Richard Cox not only ran Eton and Christ Church but, chaplain to the King, also worked for him abroad on ambassadorial missions. However the matter for which the training was most required was 'the King's Great Matter', when King Henry decided on divorce. Divorce required the consent of the head of the universal church, the Pope in Rome. The mission to establish his consent was important, difficult, and required the best canon law trained clergy that the country could provide. Two were chosen for this delicate task, both from Cambridge: Edward Fox and Stephen Gardiner. Fox was from King's, Fellow in 1515 and later frequenter of 'Little Germany'. In 1528 King Henry empowered him to negotiate with the Pope, sent him to Rome and in the same year made him Provost of King's in succession to Hacumblen, now beneath his brass.

Although Fox and Gardiner did better than might have been expected, it was almost impossible that they should succeed, given that King Henry wanted to divorce a Spanish Princess and the Spanish had the year before taken control of Rome and for a while imprisoned the Pope, giving him much more to fear from the King of Spain than he ever would from the King of England. Disconsolate, back in England, Fox and Gardiner had dinner (as one does) with another Cambridge man. This was Thomas Cranmer, who came up with the bright idea of consulting the European universities on the legitimacy of Henry's first marriage. The King approved; Fox assembled a mighty battle of arguments and the work of persuading the universities began, with Fox taking on Cambridge, Oxford, and Paris, while Croke (the University Orator from King's) took Bologna, Venice, and Padua. The result was just as unsurprising as the Pope's original decision; the universities decided according to the interests of the prevailing secular power (and in so doing rather dented the apparent objectivity of canon law).

The Pope had posed a problem which Henry resolved by declaring that England was an empire, beholden to no external authority, and replacing the Pope with himself as head of the English Church. Given the local canonical backing obtained by Fox and also having Cranmer installed as his new Archbishop, King Henry now managed to divorce his first queen and marry in her stead Anne Boleyn. Provost Fox returned to King's, the great Renaissance screen was inserted, and Fox became the first to sit in its Provost's stall (built to take a bottom of magisterial Henry VIII measurement). The screen is decorated with Anne Boleyn's symbols as well as Henry's and their initials are carved and entwined in the wood. Queen Anne only lasted a thousand days before being executed by a jealous Henry and so the screen captures an especially short punctuation point in this dynamic reign. After overseeing the later glass and conducting other diplomatic missions abroad for the King in France, Scotland, and particularly with the German Protestant princes, Fox moved on to being Bishop of Hereford in 1536; he died two years later before his incipient Protestantism could be fully tested.

We have seen how young John Frith was burnt by Henry VIII as a Protestant. Two years later he executed the aged Chancellor Fisher as a Catholic. Dexterity was needed to keep up with the royal religion and although Henry had dispensed with the Pope, he was not a Lutheran and kept the title of 'Defender of the Faith' that the Pope had granted him. (As indeed does the English monarchy to this day; it still appears on the coinage of the realm with no space on the coins to specify which faith is being defended.) The more Catholic direction of the last years of Henry's reign did not prevent continuation of his programme of dissolving the monasteries, which provided the greatest threat to the continued existence of the College (as opposed to the continued existence of its members) in this century.

In 1545 was passed 'An Act for Dissolution of Colleges'. Commissioners were appointed to evaluate colleges and chantries and take possession of them for the King. This posed a major threat to Cambridge, whose colleges were not only called 'colleges' but also seemed like colleges, that is places where people lived a communal life that incorporated daily prayer in their chapels. Part of the attraction of dissolving monasteries was loot and so a key part of deciding whether to go further in particular cases was what would be available. Hence the critical importance of the commissioners' evaluation. The result, not for the last time, revealed the creative genius of the Cambridge bursars in that only one college was returned as not making a loss (and that was Magdalene, then as now one of the less wealthy colleges). King's was returned with total expenses of £1092 against a revenue of £1010. The loss for the year was not much greater than the declared cost of the Provost, stated as £74. Of this, the Provost's annual stipend was £66, massively more than at other colleges, where it was typically £6 (Corpus, Caius, Christ's); Peterhouse paid their master an annual stipend of £2 and Clare £3. The results were inscribed on vellum and taken to the King at Hampton Court. Henry "diligently perused it and in a certain admiration said to certain of his lords which stood by that he thought that he had not in his realm so many persons so honestly maintained in living by so little land and rent." The smiling King was a good initial sign and, relying on their court contacts, the colleges survived.

King Henry, notoriously, had several wives and his three successors on the throne were his three legitimate children. Each of them was the product of a different wife and, being brought up in a different way, followed a different religion. First was Edward. He was educated by our old King's friend Cox (of Eton and Christ Church), who brought in the leading scholar of Cambridge, John Cheke, to assist him. Prince Edward therefore had the very best humanist education. However, in acquiring this, he also acquired their Protestant religion. He died young and was followed by Mary, daughter of Henry's first queen and brought up like her mother to be an impeccable Catholic. She set out with vigour to make England Catholic again. But she did not last long and it was only her successor Elizabeth who survived until old age. These accidents of dynasty and death meant England ended up as a moderately Protestant country, with bishops in direct apostolic succession as in the medieval Catholic church but not accepting either the authority of the Pope or the complete Catholic understanding of its central sacred ceremony.

After Edward Fox cashed in his State service by becoming Bishop of Hereford, the next two Provosts of King's were both from St John's. The first of them, George Day, was actually the Master of

John's before he moved. King's (as we have just seen) was better paid and men at this time moved like modern football managers between the headships of colleges; however it is probably the last time that a Master of John's would consider it a promotion becoming Provost of King's. Day fitted the more conservative last years of Henry's reign and was allowed by King Henry to keep the Provostship when he became Bishop of Chichester. He started to run into trouble, however, in the Protestant regime that followed, consistently holding a Catholic line in the House of Lords debates. He was removed as Provost, deprived of his bishopric, and imprisoned to be replaced at King's by the Protestant educator of the new Protestant King, John Cheke, Fellow of St John's.

Cheke's brother-in-law was his Johnian educated pupil, William Cecil (later Lord Burleigh) who began his distinguished career as Secretary of State in this regime. Provost Cheke also rose in the congenial new political and religious environment. He was knighted and eventually managed to combine being Provost of King's with joining Cecil as a secretary to the State Council in London. Unfortunately for him, this was exactly the wrong time to be at the centre of power and he was not as subtle as Cecil in slipping out of trouble. The young King died and the Council plotted to prevent the accession of his Catholic elder half-sister Mary by instead inserting as Queen Lady Jane Grey, who had been educated in the same Protestant circles as Edward. However, they let their prey escape; Mary learned of the death and moved out to Suffolk, staying the night in Sawston Hall as she passed near Cambridge. She declared herself the legitimate queen; there were no more sons and she was the eldest surviving daughter of Henry VIII. Secretary Cheke penned the response rejecting this on behalf of the Council and from then on he was a marked man if Mary won, as she (almost inevitably) did.

The Council equipped the Duke of Northumberland with a proper army, artillery included, to defeat the rebels (as Mary's people were in the few days of Queen Jane's reign). Northumberland came north to Cambridge (sacking Sawston Hall, tainted with Mary's mass, on the way) and lodged himself in the Provost's Lodge, the home of his friend Sir John Cheke. Here he had the use of a large house, conveniently beside the High Street and belonging to a good Protestant college. He summoned the Vice Chancellor and other heads to dinner, had the Vice Chancellor to preach a favourable sermon for him next day in Great St Mary's, and then moved his army east to Bury to hunt down the rebels, being well used from earlier in the reign to frightening revolting countrymen with artillery. The trouble this time was that Mary not only had men who had come to her help but also artillery of her own with guns taken off royal ships in a Suffolk port that had changed sides. Northumberland retreated to Cambridge and so it was in the Provost's Lodge at King's that the last act was played out of this sad short story. Back in London, the Council had changed sides and proclaimed Mary as queen. When Northumberland heard it, he did his best, hastening out into the centre of the market, throwing his cap in the air, and proclaiming Queen Mary. But it was too late and he was too prominent to turn his coat. Once back in the Provost's Lodge, he was arrested and taken under guard to London. (Given the supposed legal immunity of the College, King's was later criticised for allowing the entry of the arresting party. But the unimpeded entry of the arresting soldiers merely indicates that the College had no barrier to power in matters of national importance.)

Cheke was also arrested and taken to the Tower. From here he lasted longer than Northumberland (who was fairly promptly executed) or even Lady Jane Grey (who was not executed for a year), but his story was similarly sad. He was allowed to escape and made the continent, like many other Protestant exiles during this good Queen's reign. However, unlike them, he was trapped, brought back to England, again imprisoned in the Tower, and forced to recant. He hoped to do this privately, accepting Catholicism as the price of freedom. But he was too important an example to the regime. So it had to be done as a show trial and public recantation, from which he never really recovered. He died not long after his release from the Tower (by contrast with his brother-in-law Cecil who not only managed to work for Mary but also to become Queen Elizabeth's principal Secretary of State).

These Marian exiles, the Protestants caught up in a religiously alien regime who escaped abroad, only had to survive until 1558 before they could return home to a much happier place than Cheke. But they weren't to know it then; Mary died surprisingly young (and if she had lived as long as her sister, every subsequent part of this short history would have been different.) They gathered in Geneva and Strasbourg. In Frankfurt, the vigorous Cox managed to save the congregation from the influence of John Knox. They went to Italy. Before he was captured and brought back, Cheke (sometime Regius Professor of Greek at Cambridge) taught at the University of Padua. Among those who heard him, lecturing on Demosthenes, was another King's leading humanist and Protestant exile, Thomas Wilson. Later, back in England under Queen Elizabeth, Wilson published on Demosthenes and wrote a much used work on rhetoric as well as being for a time one of Elizabeth's secretaries of state. He assisted another Marian exile and Kingsman, Francis Walsingham, in running Elizabeth's security apparatus. It may have helped Thomas Wilson's comprehension of these delicate matters that, venturing further south in exile than Walsingham, he himself had been tortured by the Catholics in Rome.

While the Marian exiles were abroad, at home the Catholics were cleaning up the country and this included cleansing Cambridge. A commission was sent down and, given King's Protestant reputation, it was based in King's. The College had been quick enough to bring back the vestments, light the candles, and reintroduce the Catholic mass; a full Latin mass was sung in Chapel on October 1553, before it was even formally legal to do so. But the commissioners took no chances. They commandeered the Provost's and Vice Provost's stalls and had a full mass of the Holy Ghost in the Chapel to fortify themselves before the attack. They were careful what they ate in College lest they might be seduced from their serious business.

But their chief target was Great St Mary's, where the great Reformer Martin Bucer was buried. The church was placed under an interdict and only rendered suitable for worship again when holy water had been taken once right round its outside and three times round its inside. Bucer was dug up and burned in the marketplace.

He wasn't the only one, and popular memory of 'Bloody Mary', at least until recently, is seen through the prism of these burnings, graphically written up in the next reign by the martyrologist, John Foxe (whose son came to King's). It is sometimes said that in Cambridge they only burned the dead, while in Oxford they burned the living. (Another dead reformer, Fagius, was dug up from St Michael's church and burned together with Bucer.) But this is not completely correct. There was at least one Marian martyr burned alive in Cambridge and, as it happened, he was a former Scholar of King's, later a Conduct in Chapel and then Vicar of Babraham. This was John Hullier, who came to the College in 1538. It was on Maundy Thursday 1556 on Jesus Green. The fire did not take light properly, the gunpowder that had kindly been placed around his neck to speed his end failed to ignite, and Hullier had a lingering and painful death. On the fire, also being burned as part of the cleansing, were copies of the Edwardian prayer book. Hullier passed the time until his death reading the Communion Service, a dedicated disciple of the new English Book of Common Prayer. Three other former Fellows were also burned under Mary for their Protestant beliefs, although not at Cambridge.

The deprived and disgraced Cheke had to be replaced as Provost by a proper Catholic. The first replacement caught the plague while on tour collecting the College rents so a second replacement was required. This was Robert Brassey, who died at almost exactly the same time as Queen Mary and so did not have to be replaced in turn by the new Protestant power. He gave himself a chantry chapel, the next side chapel east from Hacumblen's, and here he sleeps under his brass, as if the good Catholic Church had been restored for ever and masses would continually be said for his soul. But in fact this time it really was the end. The field was clear for Queen Elizabeth and her advisers to insert a Protestant Provost as one of her first acts. Philip Baker of Barnstaple seemed to be the man, and he was elected on royal advice in 1558. Unfortunately, they got the wrong man. Baker hoarded copes and other Catholic accoutrements, ready for the next religious reversal. The Fellows appealed to the Visitor. The Visitor visited, admonished, and gave Baker a chance to repent and reform. He did not take it and just before the next cycle of visitation after a further appeal by the Fellows, he fled and went into exile abroad; he was at least decent enough to send the horses he had used for his flight back to the College.

Before he left, he had the privilege of entertaining the new queen, who came to stay in the Provost's Lodge for several days in August 1564. The Lodge was made suitable for a court and Queen Elizabeth rode into Cambridge on her horse to be greeted at the west door of the Chapel with a long Latin speech by William Master, University Public Orator and Fellow of King's. (The College's reputation for the new learning persisted through the century and not just the first but also several later Public Orators were from King's.) She listened to this patiently, still seated on her horse, before proceeding into Chapel for the service, led by the Provost, and so on out through the East End to the Lodge. In the next days she attended services, disputations, and plays, with the antechapel being adapted for the dramatic performances. Under this moderate Protestant regime, the Choir were permitted to sing again and when the Queen unexpectedly arrived late at a service, they immediately stopped and started again at the beginning.

After Provost Baker, King's elected Roger Goad, fully Protestant after Elizabethan fashion, that is prayer book and in support of episcopal government but Calvinist in doctrine with a firm belief in predestination and dependent on the doubtful solace of knowing that most of mankind were condemned to everlasting torment in hell and there was nothing anyone could do about it. Not that this stopped Goad doing a lot about things in College and University, trying to get people to sharpen up. Not for him the morality tale of the Fellow (of another college) who hanged himself with his Bible open before him at a predestination passage.

A minor aspect of these changing religious fashions was clerical marriage. The clergy thought that they could marry with Henry's first move away from the Pope, discovered that they definitely couldn't by the end of his reign, then that they definitely could (by Act of Parliament) under Edward, whereas they clearly could not with Catholic Mary. Once we reach Elizabeth, although she disliked bishops who married, marriage had come again. In Cambridge, neither clerical nor lay Fellows might marry; in King's this was part of the unalterable Founder's Statutes (but then so also were such clearly Catholic practices as saying mass daily for the Founder's soul, which were quietly forgotten). The exception was the Provost. He could, like an Elizabethan bishop, marry, even if his royal mistress disapproved. This meant that with Roger Goad, King's had for the first time a married Provost. So as well as the big Goad living in the grand house on the High Street, there was also a Mrs. Goad and numerous little Goads. And all these little Goads could in turn be recycled through Eton and back to King's, keeping more than a single generation's influence on the College.

Although King's did not, indeed could not, alter its Statutes in the way other colleges did at this time, the University Statutes written under Queen Elizabeth (and which lasted until the nineteenth century) greatly increased the power of the heads of the colleges. The government hope was that putting the heads in control would better maintain discipline, in particular religious discipline. So for the next nearly two hundred years Cambridge was run by the heads of the colleges and chief among these heads during Queen Elizabeth's reign was Goad, who was three times Vice Chancellor. And although Goad's formal position in College did not change, it no doubt helped him to increase the Provost's power as well as fitting with his bossy temperament. (Before he became Provost, he had been a headmaster.) As Vice Chancellor, he not only pursued religious deviancy, interrogating troublesome professors in the Provost's Lodge, but also produced firm rules of behaviour to keep all the University students in check, for example prohibiting games of football between different colleges. In King's, he seemed to have a particular aversion to the river. Any Scholar found to have been in the river was to be savagely flogged and any Fellow found bathing was to sit in stocks in the hall for a day.

It is accordingly not particularly surprising that Roger Goad had a sequence of fights with the Fellows of King's, which are documented in the appeals by each side to the College Visitor. Part of the difference might have been religious, part was a dispute about how to divide the income, part was a difference of temperament between the increasingly aging Goad and the much younger residing Fellows, and part was resistance to his overweening managerial style. There were riots and disorder when the Bishop of Lincoln came as Visitor to dispense peace. Application was made to Burleigh (who as well as Secretary of State was Chancellor of the University) to have recalcitrant Fellows removed. And among all the other bones of contention was Mrs. Goad. The Fellows complained to the Visitor that the Provost had allowed a woman to come into the College. Goad replied, "my wyef is not kept within the quadrant of the colledge", pointing out that they lived in convenient, set apart, lodging and that she "she neaver came twise" within "the quadrant". He also had to explain to the Visitor why he had deprived a Fellow of his free food for a week because he wore "a cut taffety dublet of the fashion, with the sleeves out, and a great payer of gallygastion hose." ('Gallygastion' is not in the OED; it's presumably Goad's spelling of 'galligaskin', first attested in the OED the year after Goad is writing and defined as "a kind of wide hose or breeches"; the man's sin seemed to have been to exchange his tights for trousers.)

Goad's children form a snapshot of what could happen to Fellows at this period. His eldest son moved to Gray's Inn, added money to what Goad gave him, had an estate in Suffolk, and (as the Statutes stipulated) left the Fellowship. His sixth son was also set up by Goad as a local landowner with an estate at Milton, at which point, again in accordance with the Statutes, he resigned his Fellowship. The estate included the presentation to the local living and Goad instructed his son to present it to his second son; this second son was the only one who took orders like his father; his clerical career included being an English representative at the Synod of Dort (in 1618, which decided the shape of subsequent Dutch religious life) and was said to have the "commanding presence" of his father. The third son matriculated in 1594 but died in College two years later. The fourth son survived longer, arriving in 1601 and becoming a Fellow in 1604. In 1609, however, he also died in College. A similar fate befell the fifth son, Fellow in 1610 and dying in 1613. So Goad had one somewhat significant son and two others who lived comfortably. Half of his six sons, however, died young in College.

They were not alone. Even people who survived to have full lives died younger and many, like Goad's sons, did not survive. Royalty presumably had the best advantages available conducive to long life. Yet of the English monarchs described in this chapter, only Queen Elizabeth survived what we (and the Bible) think of as a normal length of life and when she died at 69 she was older than any monarch in the previous 500 years. We may think of Henry VIII going on for ever, and he indeed reigned nearly 40 years, but he died at 56; Henry VII died at 52; and the monarch after Elizabeth (James I) died at 58. So established, successful, people commonly died in their fifties. Or they could have died much younger, as students, young Fellows, or the Tudor King Edward, who died at 15. (Completing the Tudor set, Queen Mary died at 42.) They died of smallpox, they died of consumption, they died of the sweating sickness, or they simply died. Some were drowned in the Cam or other rivers, which were used for washing. Some killed themselves, like William Skipton who became a Fellow in 1525. Although a priest, he associated with women in Cambridge but not in the normal manner. He liked wearing women's clothing and hanged himself in London while so dressed, supposedly in a fit of remorse for his sins.

King's had been set up like a parish with a burial ground planned by the Founder. It was exempt from episcopal jurisdiction which meant that it exercised the power of probate. People lived in College, died in College, had their wills proved by the College, and were buried in College. Lacking the Founder's planned cemetery, the burials were in the Chapel and many of these burials were not of older Fellows who had seen out their years (or had at least reached 50); they were instead of young men in their late teens or their twenties. Important people (as we have seen with the Marquess of Blandford and several Provosts) were buried in the side chapels. But the undergraduates were usually buried at the west end without a memorial while the Fellows were similarly buried at the east end. The Chapel sits on their skeletons.

CHAPTER FOUR

UNCIVIL WARS

T he reader anxious that the story of King's is no more than a
story of kings may rest assured that this is the last chapter in
which the main plot relies on the relation between a small
college in Cambridge and the ruling power in London. But before
we reach relief we still have to traverse the seventeenth century, a
century of civil wars from which the College could not be exempt.
It was for many people, including members of the College, a terrible
time. We think of the First World War as devastating slaughter, but the
English Civil Wars killed, in percentage terms, a greater proportion
of the population. Members of King's signed up in great numbers
for the First World War and, as young officers, took the greatest
rate of loss. Nevertheless, more Fellows of King's were killed in the
seventeenth century English Civil Wars than in both the twentieth
century World Wars put together. Furthermore, while the two later
World Wars were both won, King's was on the losing side of both
Civil Wars and so at the mercy of reconstruction by the victors.

For the College, this century combined the problem described
in the first chapter of connecting with the correct king with the
problem described in the last chapter of having the right religion.
This national conflict was not now between prospective kings but

between King and Parliament. But it was again a conflict about who controlled the country at a time when the College had to consort with the ruling power. In addition, although King and Parliament were both Protestant, it was in part a conflict over religion when it was still supposed, as in the last chapter, that there had to be a single religion in a single country. The high altar in the Chapel that went up and down in the last century still kept appearing and disappearing during the course of this one.

The philosopher Thomas Hobbes, who lived through it, thought that the English Civil War was caused by people reading too much Latin and Greek and becoming as a consequence excessively attached to ancient ideas about liberty. Even if this is an exaggeration, the universities that taught this Latin and Greek were too influential to be ignored. Half the Members of Parliament were from Oxford or Cambridge and when they met they criticised the universities (or engaged in acrimonious dispute about which was older). The Crown controlled appointments, writing to "our college in our university at Cambridge" about the right man to elect as Provost of King's, and the College always did what it was told. When the Crown was replaced by Parliament, it became even more concerned about who should be heads of colleges. As the nursery of the people who held power in a contentious and conflicted period, with people killing each other for their political and religious beliefs, Cambridge and King's were inevitably of concern to those holding political and religious power.

Allegiance was accordingly important. It was a time of loyalties, and conflicting loyalties. It was a time of oaths, since there was a general presupposition that loyalty could be procured by people swearing allegiance. So oaths (made before the divine, all-seeing, punishing God) were applied to anyone whose allegiance was significant, including all Fellows of Cambridge colleges. The century started, after the Catholic Gunpowder Plot to blow up King and Parliament, with everyone having to swear that they were not Catholics. Then, later, when Parliament and King fall out and

Parliament defeated the King, oaths were administered to the Fellows by the Parliamentary victors. First they had to swear they had the right sort of Protestantism and then a few years later, after the King has been executed, a second round of oaths was applied, when the Fellows had to swear loyalty to Parliament as the legitimate government of the country, foreswearing all belief in kings. But then this eternal and sworn correct form of government collapsed, allowing the executed King's son to return. Royalty was now right and further oaths of loyalty were administered to the Fellows, this time in favour of the new king.

At each stage, refusing the oath (or failing to appear) entailed expulsion. So flexibility and foresight were required to continue holding a Fellowship and the successive rounds caused anguish to scrupulous individuals. In the restoration of monarchy oath the Fellows swore that they were under no obligation arising from their earlier oaths, since (as the text they read out helpfully explained) these were illegal oaths. But similarly for all the previous commitments. At each stage, the next revolution of government brought in by fortune's wheel could invalidate previous performances. But in the meantime Fellows were anguished, deprived, and might not live long enough to be restored. The century ends (after another shuffle of kings to make sure that they stayed Protestant) with another set of oaths to the new monarchy. A group (the 'Non Jurors'), felt bound by their earlier allegiance, refused to swear, and so lost their positions. In St John's College this led to a large loss of Fellows, but in King's, after a century of conflicting oaths, they were all happy to swear and stay.

In the first forty years of the century this anguish was as yet unknown and the College continued on its serene course, as described before and as if inexorably for ever. The sanctified number of seventy on the Foundation, as prescribed by the Founder, was respected and the Provost and two Fellows acting as 'Posers' went annually to Eton to elect Scholars to make up the number. The elected were then admitted when vacancies occurred, so that every particular Scholar coming in arrived because of a particular Fellow (or Scholar) going out. As before, the Fellows left because they took on parishes or got married. Or died. Smallpox and consumption still culled them in significant numbers, creating vacancies, although the sweating sickness disappeared as mysteriously as it had arrived. Plague cleared the town and episodically prevented teaching. There was still some drowning. And the occasional more unusual deaths occurred like the young Fellow who attended a cock fight in the Blue Boar and laughed so much that he died.

This was the maximum period for undergraduate numbers in addition to the Scholars on the Foundation; indeed it is the only time before the late nineteenth century that there were more non-Scholar than Scholar undergraduates. The University, similarly, was at a size that it didn't recover for centuries. The additional undergraduates at King's weren't necessarily from a different background from the Scholars, as the College was flexible in using the positions of Scholar Commoner and Fellow Commoner. Boys from Eton elected as Scholars but waiting for a vacancy would come and wait in Cambridge until it appeared. They were often pensioners at other colleges, transferring to King's once one of the magic seventy had left. But they were also Scholar Commoners or Fellow Commoners in King's itself while they waited their turn. The Civil War deprivations just described did not only apply to Fellows; they also applied to former Fellows who lost their parishes. One of the most distinguished of these was John Pearson, probably the greatest scholar before Bentley in seventeenth century Cambridge. Having lost his parish, he returned to King's and although ineligible to be a Fellow again he lived in College as a Fellow Commoner. His life was very like that of a formal Fellow, including giving University sermons. (With the Restoration of the Monarchy, he became Bishop of Chester and was known to centuries of later theological students as 'Pearson on the Creed'.) Similar flexibility could be applied to undergraduates; one at this period who got married (and thereby automatically lost his Scholarship) was permitted by the College to continue as a Fellow Commoner until he graduated.

Presiding over the College from 1615 was the scholarly and witty figure of Samuel Collins, whose memorial inscription we saw in the Hacumblen Chapel. Provost of King's, the only Kingsman to be Regius Professor of Divinity (until someone was imported at the end of the nineteenth century as one of the new Professorial Fellows), keeping abreast of Bacon and the new learning, the College was in distinguished hands. The Regius Professor of Physic (that is, Medicine) was also from King's (and he wasn't the only one; the College kept the medical reputation that it had at the start, with four of the first nine professors being from King's). So was the Regius Professor of Civil Law (and, again, not the only one from the College; here four of the first twelve were from King's, but after this they were all for centuries from Trinity Hall).

It might be thought that a book called *A new Gagg for an old Goose* would not cause much trouble. However, written by former Fellow Richard Montague, it became a centre of conflict between King and Parliament, twenty years before the Civil War started. Periodically Parliament met, complained about this and other sores, and got dissolved by the King. Eventually, King Charles I managed to dispense with it altogether and rule without its trouble for eleven years, only having to recall it when he needed money to fight the Scots and thereafter getting into so much trouble from Parliament that it led to civil war between them. Parliament, both earlier and later, was concerned that the Court and bishops were trying to turn England back in a more Catholic direction, away from the earlier prevailing moderate Puritanism (as had been represented by Provost Goad at King's). The new trend in religion was termed 'Arminianism'. It was defeated in Arminius's own Dutch home (at the Synod of Dort where Goad Junior was a delegate). But it increased in influence in England, particularly once William Laud had replaced Goad's old pupil Abbot as Archbishop of Canterbury. Montague tried to defend himself against the charge of Arminianism by protesting that he had not read a word of Arminius. But this was no good; the flavour of his thought was too sympathetic to Catholicism and

Parliament, each time it met, wanted him imprisoned and his books burnt. The new king somewhat incautiously defended him, excused him by royal prerogative, dissolved the angry Parliament, and made Montague a bishop.

The chief conceptual division between the Arminians and their Puritan or Parliamentary opponents was support for an element of choice on the road to salvation, as opposed to Calvinist predestination. But more important than what people thought was what people did: candles came back in church, as did the high altars to which people started bowing. The leading Cambridge colleges in such Catholic chapel refurbishment were Caius and Peterhouse. But in King's, Collins returned the high altar and started to bow. So when the Parliamentarians won, he was a marked man. He tried to anticipate trouble and removed the altar in King's Chapel even before Parliament ordered it. But it was too late and he had shown too much of his hand; come the revolution, he was ejected as Provost.

On the other side of the religious argument was Emmanuel College, breeder of Puritans such as the Cambridge men who renamed a place 'Cambridge' in Massachusetts and founded Harvard; Harvard himself was from Emmanuel. The Master of Emmanuel, and leading Puritan in Cambridge in the first part of the century, was John Preston. He had started at King's as a Sizar. This had given him a love of music but he'd moved to a college where, unlike King's, he had a chance of becoming a Fellow. It was Preston who led for the opposition when Montague was examined in London. Later, after Parliament had won the Civil War, it was Puritan Emmanuel men who were used to replace the ejected heads of other colleges, including the replacement for Collins at King's.

When everything fell apart for the King in 1642 and he left London to start war against Parliament, he came with his son and heir (the later Charles II) through Cambridge on his way to raise his standard at Nottingham. First he was cautious and stayed out of town, letting his son represent him. The young Charles was received by the Provost and it was remarked how he prayed openly in the

Chapel, not hiding his head in his hat. The teenager was so positively received by the town that his royal father came back with him next day. The chief celebrations were elsewhere, but they were presented with a Bible by the Provost. Then, after a buffet lunch at John's, they set off up the hill and out by the Huntingdon Road away to start the war, cheered on by the townspeople lining the street.

A little later the people gathered in the same street, expecting to see the sight of the plate of the Cambridge colleges being taken under armed guard to be melted down in support of the King's military effort. (Parliament controlled the City of London and the King needed finance from elsewhere to compete.) But the event did not happen and the assembled populace was disappointed. Now with two sides in conflict, there are two stories about what actually happened, each with its rival spin. It's clear that King Charles wrote to the Cambridge colleges, requesting their plate. It's clear that it (or at least some of it) was brought together in King's from the other colleges and it's clear that Docwra came with his armed men, colours flying and drums beating, to King's to provide its armed guard. It would have been a splendid sight for the waiting populace on Castle Hill. However Docwra got no further than King's, interrupted by a local man of unusual energy and drive, one Oliver Cromwell. Cromwell, who was MP for the city, did not content himself with waiting with his hastily gathered irregular forces out at Lolworth to intercept the plate. He came into town and besieged King's, which hastily shut the old gatehouse against him.

It is here that the stories diverge. The Royalist story is that the wily President of Clare, who knew the back roads, spirited the plate away the night before Cromwell's advance, and certainly some Cambridge plate reached the King. The Parliamentary story, as inscribed on the Parliamentary rolls, is that Oliver Cromwell was congratulated for his initiative in preventing the transport of the plate and retrospectively excused for acting before he had been given Parliamentary authority to do so, and certainly some plate reached Parliament. Some college plate went neither route; Jesus, for example, simply buried it in their garden for ten years. We don't know about what happened to the King's plate (although the most likely story is that some college plate got to the King and some did not) but we do know that the College had a relatively low profile. The Masters of John's, Queens', and Jesus, who were conspicuous royal supporters, were taken into custody and firstly imprisoned in the Tower and later in hulks. They had a horrible time. Whereas Provost Collins was simply subsequently deprived of his office and managed to live out his life in a decent house on Jesus Lane.

King's had a lower Royalist profile than some other colleges, but once the war started it was on the side of the King. Several Fellows of the College fought in the royal army. They include: James Ayre, killed at Berkeley Castle in 1645; Henry Bard, who was a colonel, knighted, and Governor of Worcester; William Raven, captain of a troop of horse; William Rose (or Rosse), who died in service in 1643; Tobias Hodson, a major in a regiment of horse; Henry Pearce, who was wounded at Bridgewater in 1645 and died of his wounds; and Charles Howard, another captain of a troop of horse, who was slain near Newark in 1645. Sampson Biggs had been a Fellow for ten years when he was killed in 1643 at the siege of Gloucester. William Fairbrother, Fellow since 1633, served in the royal army and was taken prisoner at Naseby in 1645; when he was released after being imprisoned in London, he lived the rest of his life in College as a Fellow, becoming Vice Provost. Another Fellow who served, was captured, and returned to College was John Woodhall. Arthur Swayne, a Fellow killed while serving for the King, was more unfortunate. When teaching his servant to handle a musket one day in the Royalist headquarters in Oxford, he failed to realise that it was loaded. He was buried in 1644 in Oxford Cathedral.

These were all still Fellows; the number goes up if we include former Fellows or undergraduates, such as John Pradman, who served as a lieutenant in the Royalist army as a Scholar of the College and only became a Fellow at the war's end in 1646. Dore Williamson, Fellow from 1627-34 had left College to become a rector; he nevertheless signed up for the King and lost a leg to a cannon ball at Newark in 1646. These clerics did not mind fighting but there were also clerics who acted as chaplains, such as James Fleetwood who was so effective the night before the Battle of Edgehill (or at least so successful in leading people to think that he was) that he was created an Oxford DD by the King, using his royal mandate, on returning to the Royalist capital.

I can trace no Fellow who similarly fought in the Parliamentary armies. But, after Parliament won, clear supporters of the other side emerged. There was Thomas Almond, described as the 'delator', who informed on Fellows refusing to show loyalty to the new masters. And there was Anthony Ascham. Ascham, who became a Fellow in 1637, was a clear supporter of Parliament. It is not clear what role he played in the war but he was a powerful propagandist for the Parliamentary cause after the war, writing several books arguing for conformity to Parliament as the politically effective power; government, he held, comes from the people. He paid for this progressive thought with his life, being assassinated by Royalists in Madrid in 1650 when on a mission there for his new Parliamentary masters.

The Fellows might mainly have declared for the King, but King's was from the start and throughout the war in a part of the country controlled by Parliament. After Cromwell's early initiative in stopping the plate, he organised Cambridge (for which he was the Member of Parliament) to become the strong point of the Eastern Association of the Parliamentary army. Castle Hill was fortified and the bridges (including King's) were removed to make the town easier to defend. It was never in fact near serious fighting (although there was a bit of a panic when the Royalists took Huntingdon late in the war), but it felt close to the front line. The town was full of soldiers and when it was wet they paraded inside King's Chapel; the College had more than once to resort to bribes in an attempt to make them behave themselves.

Just as the King in the previous century, over-riding the Statutes, had given King's a more distinguished Provost from outside than it could have produced itself, so also a century later. Then the King had produced Cheke to further the Protestant cause; now, to a similar end, Parliament produced Benjamin Whichcote. Collins, Regius Professor, was distinguished and home grown but Whichcote, who had no previous connection with the College before he became Provost in 1645, was one of the group of influential thinkers we call the Cambridge Platonists. He had a significant effect on the religious life of England both now and also later in the second half of the century, when Archbishop of Canterbury Tillotson commented that he "contributed more to the forming of the students [and] to a sober sense of Religion than any man in that Age". He was also an exceedingly wise head in piloting the College through the difficult waters of civil wars and Parliamentary innovation, as well as managing to deprive the odious tale-teller Almond of his Fellowship.

In fact Whichcote was so respected that he is often given the credit for things that were accidental or had other causes. One such is the survival of the Chapel glass. This is indeed a puzzle when the iconoclastic Parliamentary Puritans were in charge and the godly soldiers were parading in the Chapel before fighting against bishops wishing to restore the beauty of holiness and reintroduce Catholic images. A Suffolk yeoman, William Dowsing, made it his godly mission to rid East Anglia of anything 'Romish'. He toured East Anglia, including the Cambridge colleges, removing what he called superstitious images and smashing superstitious glass. So how did the King's Chapel glass survive? Dowsing came, but he did not destroy and the only damage the Chapel experienced throughout this period was the defacement of Marian supporters for the door arches in the choir. The apparently miraculous survival of the glass has been attributed to Whichcote's magic, charming Dowsing out of casting the first stone. But more likely it was an accident, and in any case Dowsing visited before Whichcote became Provost. (Another believed, but even less likely, story is that the windows were all removed in a single night before Dowsing arrived.)

On his Cambridge visit, Dowsing made a hasty tour of the colleges, usually enlisting a pliant Fellow in support and removing a statue here or an image there. When he reached King's, it was December 26th 1643. Being Boxing Day would not have led to any lack of effort as God-fearing Puritans wanted to abolish Christmas. (Ironically in that God-fearing age nothing stopped for the Christian feast of Christmas whereas in our own atheist times nothing moves for a week.) In his diary Dowsing writes about the visit: "one thousand superstitious pictures, the ladder of Christ, and thieves to go on many crosses, and Jesus writ on them." This reads to me like a man who sees that there is simply too much to do and notes to himself that he needs to come back and make a proper job of it (but never did). Anyone destroying the glass would have had to arrange an alternative means of filling the windows to make Cambridge's largest building still suitable for drilling soldiers or other purposes. But this alone would not have saved it. King Henry VII's Chapel in Westminster Abbey was filled with a similar amount of glass of a similar period and installed for similar purposes. (The same King; the same memorial project.) Yet none of it survives; it was all smashed during this Parliamentary period. So it is fortunate that we can still see King Henry VII's project in Cambridge even if no longer in London.

The first round of oaths (that is, the examination and expulsion of Fellows) was in 1644, before the first Civil War was won but after Dowsing had passed through. This examination was mainly on religious grounds, whereby anyone holding an official position had to sign up to the Solemn League and Covenant agreed by Parliament with the Scots. The Earl of Manchester was appointed to oversee the business and removed most of the remaining heads of colleges. He presented Whichcote to the vacancy at King's and ejected eight Fellows of King's for refusing to swear.

The second round of oaths was after Parliament had won the second Civil War and executed the King. This was primarily political rather than religious. Fellows had to swear that government by parliament rather than by king was the only legitimate form of government. This oath (known as 'The Engagement') caused a lot of difficulty to the remaining Fellows. Some of the other newly introduced heads at other colleges were turned out again at this stage and even Manchester himself was removed for refusing the Engagement. The Master and entire Fellowship of St Catharine's was removed. This did not happen at King's. There were very few expulsions, although they did remove the University Orator. Here it does seem that Whichcote did manage to work some magic, particularly since it would seem that neither he nor most of the Fellows actually took the oath (and, as I noted at the start, non-appearance did not save someone; the Orator was expelled for failing to appear.) Provost Whichcote's first try was to write "as we had adhered to Parliament, so we would live peaceably not disturbing the present government, desiring this might be accepted for our subscription." In other words, he claimed that their actions showed that they accepted the prevailing power and so no explicit declaration was required. This was not usually sufficient but somehow, one way or the other, he seems to have worked it.

And so eventually (although this would have been to everyone's surprise after the King was executed and Whichcote was wriggling), fortune's wheel made another revolution and the man who hadn't hid in his hat to pray in Chapel returned as King Charles II. More oaths. More pertinently, both Whichcote himself and also the Fellows wished him to continue as Provost. Nor was this impossible; his fellow Cambridge Platonist, Cudworth, introduced as Master of Christ's by the Parliamentarians, managed to survive as Master after the royal restoration. But Whichcote ran into trouble in the shape of James Fleetwood, created DD by Charles I for what he was supposed to have done before the Battle of Edgehill and now a royal chaplain. Fleetwood went to see the new king and managed (on the basis of past services rendered to the right side) to persuade him to tell the Fellows of King's to elect him as Provost. Which they duly did. There were various subsequent arguments, one strand of which was the claim that the election was illegal since by the Statutes an election had to be within fifteen days of the vacancy and yet the vacancy (on one way of looking at it) had occurred sixteen years before when Collins was ejected. Whichcote's servants in the Provost's Lodge refused admission to Fleetwood when he arrived to take possession, so he had to return to his royal master for further powers. However Whichcote, his point having been made, then made a dignified retreat and went to preach in London with great and persistent effect.

Nor was the preaching only in London. In Cambridge the University naturally wished to celebrate the Restoration of the Monarchy and called on a Fellow of King's to do the deed with a sermon in the University Church. And so on 24 May 1660 in Great St Mary's "Will. Godman B.D., Fellow of the King's College in Cambridge" preached on the "day of solemn thanksgiving for the deliverance and settlement of our nation." Then, duty done and no longer troubled by the great events of the realm, the College happily settled down to a century and a half of slumber.

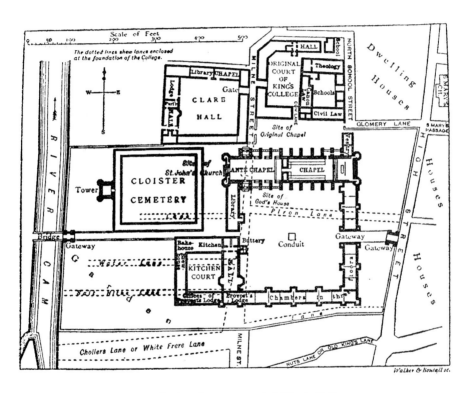

Henry VI's plan for an expanded King's College.
A. Austen Leigh, *King's College* (1899), p.17.

PROFES. IOANNES CHECUS
GRÆ. LINGUA CHECVS EQUES
AVRATVS

Ingenium magni moderatus Principis exul
CHECVS, at inconstans in pietate fuit AB

John Cheke, Provost 1549–1553.
© National Portrait Gallery, London.

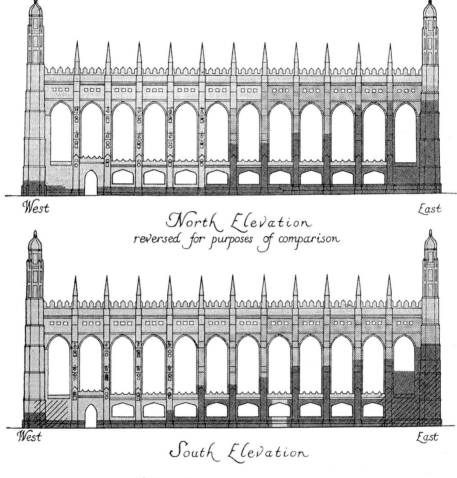

West   East

North Elevation
reversed for purposes of comparison

West   East

South Elevation

KING'S COLLEGE CHAPEL

Diagrammatic Sketch indicating the Building progress

▇ *Founder's work 1446~61* ▨ *Probably completed by 1485* ☐ *1508-1515*

▨ *Refacing*

Progress in building the Chapel. Royal Commission
on Historical Monuments, *City of Cambridge* (1959), I, p.100.

Charles Simeon, Fellow 1782-1836.
College Archives: KCAC/1/4/Simeon.

Old Provost's Lodge. R. Willis, J. W. Clark,
The Architectural History of the University of Cambridge (1886), I, p.548.

Richard Okes, Provost 1850-1889.
College Archives: KCAC/1/4/Okes.

Old Court by H.S. Storer.
Modern Archives: JS/4/13/3.

Tess Adkins, Fellow 1972-, Senior Tutor 1981-1995, Acting Provost 2005-2006.
College Archives: Coll Ph 217. Photo by Edward Leigh.

CHAPTER FIVE

OLD CORRUPTION

T he last successful invasion of England was by the Dutch in
1689. The admiral who was meant to stop them landing was
a Kingsman and wished to do so; however he was resisted by
his captains who let them through. When the Dutch King William
got to land, the army sent to resist him similarly would not fight.
Hence the so-called 'Bloodless Revolution' because blood was not
spilt in England; naturally the plentiful blood spilt in Ireland and
Scotland did not count. The bloodless revolution in the country also
led to a bloodless revolution at King's in which the College finally
gained control of its own affairs. We saw in previous chapters how
the prevailing national power not only selected the bishops (including
several from King's) but also the heads of Cambridge colleges. In each
case, there was a local formal electing body but in each case it was
instructed in its choice by the Crown. The arrival of the new Dutch
King coincided with a vacancy in the Provostship. Initially the new
King attempted to fill it in the same old way, informing the College
that his royal will was that they elect Isaac Newton as Provost. However
the College resisted and achieved the reality rather than the mere form
of electing according to its Statutes; both on this occasion and also
for ever after, it freely elected whoever the Fellows chose as Provost.

That is the short story. A slightly longer version would note that the imposition of outsiders, who (contrary to the Statutes) had no previous connection with King's, had produced the most academically distinguished Provosts to grace the College. As we have seen, these included Cheke (previously Fellow of John's) and Whichcote (previously Fellow of Emmanuel). Newton (Fellow of Trinity) would have trumped both of these; he had just published *Principia* and was at the height of his powers and reputation. Nor should he be thought to be an unworldly academic unsuitable for administration; he was at this time MP for Cambridge and later became a highly effective Warden and later Master of the Royal Mint in London. Newton would have been a catch. But the College did not get Newton, nor, for centuries, anyone remotely like him. Instead, left free to its devices, the College proceeded to elect academic nonentities from its own stock and disappeared into centuries of slumber. It was two hundred years before it once more considered electing an academically distinguished outsider and, having considered it, decided not to do it, rejecting once again the Fellow of Trinity and electing someone safely undistinguished of its own. And although academically impressive Provosts were eventually elected in the twentieth century, the College had to wait until the twenty-first before it freely elected an outsider.

These short stories are significant but in fact we need a somewhat longer story to understand the 1689 election and the College's subsequent freedom. King William was taking over an alien country, intent on securing his new crown, and gearing up to fight France, the greatest power in Europe. He had more pressing concerns than who was in charge of a Cambridge college. Also, although this would not at first have been apparent, Oxford and Cambridge were becoming less important nationally and so of less concern to the Court. Theological position mattered less for national politics, providing less need to control the seminaries; analogously, the landed families, several of whose sons would achieve power, became less interested in sending them to universities. In

Cambridge, numbers reduced to about half what they had been in the early seventeenth century and King's shrank back to just its Scholars, similarly losing the additional students who had earlier doubled its undergraduate size.

The royal interest in the 1689 election in fact started not in the Court but in the College. An ambitious Fellow, John Hartcliffe, rode to the Court to inform it of its traditional right of nomination (and no doubt suggesting how to use it). Alerted, the Court summoned College representatives to a conference at the royal palace in Hampton Court. The traditional account is that the King first came up with the name of a Fellow of Eton and only when this proved unacceptable switched to Isaac Newton; most but not all modern accounts have the King promoting Newton from the start. Both accounts could be correct; the Court records show that the King settled immediately on Newton, but he could initially have tried for tactical reasons someone known to be unacceptable. In any case the main argument was about Newton and was sufficiently vigorous (with one of the Fellows being very deaf and very loud) that the Queen elsewhere in the palace was worried that the revolution was ceasing to be bloodless. The Fellows rejected Newton because, as a Fellow of Trinity, his election would be contrary to the Statutes. After the conference, the King wrote to the College mandating that they elect John Hartcliffe, who had initiated the whole process.

No doubt the King thought he was being clever, giving King's one of its own Fellows but preserving the traditional royal power of nomination. But by now the ambitious Hartcliffe was detested inside the College and the Fellows resisted the royal command and instead elected another Fellow, Charles Roderick. (It was not unanimous; Hartcliffe voted for himself and he was not alone.) There was then a nasty stalemate, with the King and College holding on while considerable behind the scenes diplomacy was applied by his advisors to make the King give way. In the end a form of amicable agreement between Crown and College was acted out in public. Ground prepared, the King visited King's on his way to the races at Newmarket and the Fellows on their knees begged him in the Chapel to be so kind as to allow them to elect in accordance with their Statutes, to which he graciously consented. What worried the advisors (and could have worried Parliament if it went that far) was that the King had ostensibly invaded to restore liberty unlike his predecessor who used the royal prerogative to over-ride established laws and procedures. One of King James II's last acts before he was deposed was to attempt the replacement of the Fellows of Magdalen College Oxford with Catholics. He had earlier caused concern in Cambridge by instructing that a Catholic friar be given a degree; prominent in opposition to this was Isaac Newton, who wrote in protest against the idea of royal power fixing Cambridge positions.

Finally free, the College elected the Fellow who was Headmaster of Eton, which, even apart from the lack of academic distinction, was rather a bad idea. And he wasn't the only one; in the eighteenth century, the College elected three headmasters of Eton in a row as Provost, only switching in the nineteenth century to the Lower Master at Eton (when it elected two in a row). Every Fellow had been to Eton and the Fellows who had been under his rod presumably saw their old headmaster as a figure of authority. This one was described by a perceptive contemporary observer as "a very disagreeable instance how far an affectation of gravity and a studied formality may transport a man." As well as his over-formal, cold, style, he was excessively interested in preventing and punishing minor peccadillos; in short, a headmaster come to King's. The same unenthused contemporary noted that he knew boys but did not understand men. However Charles Roderick understood enough to succeed in the normal run of preferment, acquiring additional ecclesiastical appointments (and income), becoming rector of several parishes and eventually Dean of Ely. He even got married not many years before he died in the Provost's Lodge. But he was so shy that he could never in his life summon up the nerve to ascend a pulpit to read out his own previously written sermons. And this is the man that the College preferred to Newton; this is the man who as Vice

Chancellor expelled Newton's friend, follower, and successor in the Lucasian Chair (William Whiston) from the University for heresy.

With the College falling back into itself for the century and a half with which this chapter deals, this was the time of closest connection between Eton and King's. When the Fellows completed their Front Court early in the nineteenth century, they naturally adorned the outside of their new Porters Lodge with the arms of the College. Equally naturally, they gave a similar position to the arms of Eton. (King's is on the left, looking from King's Parade, Eton on the right.) The additional students from other backgrounds disappeared and the College was solely composed of the sacred seventy Etonians. Charles Roderick was not unusual in being a Kingsman who went back to teach at Eton, becoming first Lower Master, then Headmaster, while continuing to hold his King's Fellowship. Etonians came to King's and Kingsmen taught at Eton while still continuing as Fellows of King's. Those who were particularly lucky eventually managed to transfer to a Fellowship at Eton, which paid more and where (unlike King's) a Fellow might be married as well as holding his Fellowship together with a well-remunerated Vicarage.

It ran in families. The sons of King's Scholars at Eton became King's Scholars in turn before they followed their fathers to become Scholars and Fellows of King's. Old corruption it could be called. We can see how it worked in the memoirs of W C Green, which he published in 1905. Green mainly lived in the new world described in the next chapter when this system was superseded. However he started in the old world. Born in 1836 at Eton, his first remembered home was the Cloisters in Eton College. His father was a Fellow of Eton and the Cloisters (that is, the back court now occupied by Headmaster, Bursary, and Vice Provost) were where the Eton Fellows then lived with their families. The man living next door, just like his father, had been a Fellow of King's until his marriage. Their sons grew up together, played together in the Eton college garden, became King's Scholars at Eton and so came to King's.

A small closed world. And the numbers were tiny. We can get a sense of this, again from near the end of its operation, in the diary of Joseph Romilly, who was the University Registrary from 1832. One October day in 1850, after matriculating the new first year University students, he notes the numbers. There were 129 new first years at Trinity; there were three at King's. This was in fact an especially large year overall for King's admissions. We have seen how Scholars were admitted whenever a vacancy arose and in this year of 1850 one was admitted in February, one in March, and two on different days in April, as well as the three Romilly matriculated in October; seven in all. In the following years the numbers admitted were: 4, 4, 7, 6, 1, 6, 5, 3, and 4, making an average of less than five undergraduates a year. Similarly at the start of the century; in the decade from 1800 to 1809 forty-three were admitted, or a little over four a year. On another occasion, Romilly notes how he was asked when the last man matriculated from King's who was not on the Foundation. He consulted the records and found that it was 1810, over forty years before. Even for those hoping to become Scholars on the Foundation, there were fewer vacancies than before, partly because of vaccination against smallpox and the disappearance of the plague, and partly because there was less tendency simply to leave. Stratagems had sometimes to be employed. Fellows were bribed to resign. Someone seeking a place for his son informed the College that a Fellow kept a house elsewhere with a woman and children and so should be removed, being (as the College described such cases) 'a married man according to the spirit of the College Statutes'.

The Statutes never could have been kept once Catholicism had departed and the whole structure given up for which the College had been founded of masses for the dead. Yet the College ferociously believed that it held to its Founder's Statutes and the Fellows believed that they were under oath not to alter them. So no one could be a Scholar or Fellow who was not from Eton, and no one could hold a Fellowship who was married or had an ecclesiastical benefice. The third cause of removal, having an estate of a certain value, was more obscure as allowance had to be made for inflation. Another attempt to get rid of a Fellow and cause a vacancy was when he was accused of having an estate, to which he replied that he'd resign when it made some money. Even the saintly Simeon (of whom more later) was sensitive about this after he had inherited family money; he justified retaining his Fellowship on the basis that he gave the income to charity and so was only holding the money in trust. For a man dressing well and keeping a fine horse, had he not been a saint this would have skirted hypocrisy.

The College in fact also relaxed observation of the Statutes with respect to residence. The Founder said that Scholars and Fellows had to reside in College. However Fellows were increasingly allowed to hold their Fellowships while living or working elsewhere. As we have seen, Assistant Masters at Eton continued to hold their King's Fellowships. An elected Fellow might proceed to the Inns of Court in London to learn the English law, all the while retaining his Fellowship; he could continue holding it to supplement his subsequent legal earnings as long as he did not commit the cardinal sin of matrimony. And although Fellows could not become Vicars or Rectors, they could become chaplains. So ambitious ecclesiastics were chaplains to bishops or peers, while holding their Fellowships. We saw in the second chapter how Francis Hare was a Fellow of King's while Chaplain-General with Marlborough's army in Flanders. The College was also extremely relaxed about Fellows incarcerated in madhouses, of whom there were several in this period. They continued as Fellows, drawing the dividend from their Fellowships, and in due course became Senior Fellows with increased salaries even though confined to Bedlam or county asylum.

This all resulted in an even smaller college actually on the ground in Cambridge. A comparison with Trinity in the early 1840s showed 30 in residence at King's, compared with 351 at Trinity. Therefore less than half of the statutory seventy were actually there. The ones who were comprised: Provost, Vice Provost, 13 MA Fellows, 5 BA Fellows, and 10 undergraduates. The undergraduates had to keep residence (just as they also, unlike the Fellows, had to go to daily services in Chapel). So only a third of the Fellows were in residence.

This long century of a very small college may seem retrospectively strange but it was not completely static or without value. It was the period during which the College had its only Prime Minister (Walpole), its only Archbishop of Canterbury (Sumner), and its most influential religious figure (Simeon). It was also the time during which the College broke out of the bounds of its accidental Old Court and finally achieved the court that the Founder had planned centuries before. Also, although it might be described as a long slumber in retrospect, it didn't feel like this to those who were there in the first half of the eighteenth century. This was the period of political parties and King's caught the disease in a particularly virulent form. After the regime change of 1713, power was for over forty years with the party called the Whigs, embodied by Kingsman and Britain's first Prime Minister, Robert Walpole. It might seem strange that a local squire like Walpole was at King's. But the answer is that he was a second son, and so educated as a Scholar at Eton and hence King's, while his elder brother was groomed to take over the estate. As soon as his brother died, he left the College, although still an undergraduate, to take over his new responsibilities. But he continued to care for his old college (which, with Eton, had given him sufficient Latin to converse as Prime Minister with his German King). To fit in with power, as it had done before, the College would have been advised to stay Whig and cultivate this connection. However it instead elected someone from the other party, the Tories, and after the election of the Tory Andrew Snape in 1720, the Provost was removed from preferment and there was incessant wrangling between the supporters of two national parties inside the house. It was not a happy college and it was too agitated to be properly asleep.

This culminated in the election for Snape's successor in 1743, which was fought on strictly party lines (and of which we have, luckily, an eye-witness account). The trouble was that there were three candidates, two Whigs and a Tory, which meant that there was difficulty in securing a majority of the electors for any candidate. Then, as now, election was in the Chapel. The Fellows went in on a Monday morning and were caught there until well into the following day once (after prayers and sacraments) a 22:16:10 split was revealed. Walking, eating, smoking, sleeping, but held all of a frosty February night in the unheated Chapel. The eye-witness account describes them at 2 a.m.: "some, wrapped in blankets, erect in their stalls like mummies; others asleep on cushions like so many Gothic tombs", with others drinking brandy. Eventually the supporters of the two rival Whig candidates managed to combine and make an election. (Surprise, surprise, they decided to elect the Headmaster of Eton.) Attached again to the Whig gravy train, the new Provost some years later became Dean of Lincoln. Not that, of course, this additional office and stipend gave him any reason for resigning as Provost; it merely meant that when the Visitor (the Bishop of Lincoln) visited the College he also had an opportunity of meeting the dean of his cathedral.

Ever since its saintly Founder disappeared before he'd finished the job, the College had wanted to complete his planned great court. As described in the first chapter, it had built nothing beyond the Chapel and had to make do for accommodation with its crammed Old Court and palatial Provost's Lodge. However in the supposedly somnolent period covered by the current chapter, the remaining three sides of the Founder's planned great court were completed. This happened in two waves. In the first half of the eighteenth century, the Gibbs Building was constructed on its west side. A hundred years later the Chapel, which had already stood for over four centuries on the north side, was finally matched by a hall and accommodation on the south side. At the same time the court was completed with a screen on its east side.

The start of the initiative that eventually led to the Gibbs Building came from outside the College. It wasn't a royal initiative, as it had been in the College's first century. However the plan was

once again to use royal finance, building a King's College not only fit
for kings but also funded by them. Lord Dartmouth, a former Fellow
Commoner of the College, stood well with the King and thought
that he could persuade him to fund the completion of the Founder's
plan. Unfortunately, the king in question was the King James who
was soon after chased away from the Crown and unable to contribute.
Unfortunately, Lord Dartmouth was the admiral described above
who failed to prevent the chasing and was therefore imprisoned
for attempting to assist the losing side. Therefore neither King nor
go-between was any longer in a position to do the job and the idea
lapsed. Roderick, the Provost who came in with the new Dutch king,
was more interested in fiddling once again with the Chapel altar.
So court completion had to wait until the advent of his successor
John Adams in 1712. But once in post Provost Adams attacked the
matter with vigour. He started a building fund and arranged for
the College to fell and sell trees to feed it. The central plan was still
royal and Adams kept angling for a meeting with the monarch (now
Queen Anne) to secure royal funding. Queen Anne died before he
could close in and there was a gap before he eventually secured a
meeting with her successor (the German George I). An informal
understanding had been reached that the King would come up with
a serious offer of money at the meeting but, unfortunately, this time
it was Provost Adams who suddenly died just before it was to take
place. No meeting, no royal money, and so ended the last attempt to
have King's built by kings.

Without royal support, the College had to turn to the people,
tapping friends and alumni. For this, both then and later, King's was
relatively poorly provided. We saw above how few students came to
King's, as compared to Trinity or John's. Also, the few it had, taking
a scholarly route through Eton and King's, were rarely from landed
or seriously moneyed families. (Aristocracy might have their sons
educated at Eton, but not as poorly fed and housed Scholars on King
Henry VI's foundation.) And even if the royal deal had gone through,
the King would only have come up with £2000, which would have

still left most of the funds to be found elsewhere. The next Provost, Andrew Snape, took up the task in 1720, without royal assistance and further retarded by the bursting of the South Sea Bubble that year, which hit the funds of both the College and possible donors. As a prominent Tory when the Whigs were firmly in power, he was not best placed to tap the winning side. However he pressed for donations and did manage to pull in two of his Tory friends. The Earl of Anglesea and John Hungerford each subscribed £100, although neither had any previous connection with the College.

It was also early enough in the century for there still to be some former Fellow Commoners (in a way there would not have been later) for whom the College was more important than the party of the Provost. So Prime Minister Robert Walpole came in handsomely with £500. His Norfolk neighbour, brother-in-law, fellow member of the Whig administration, and former Fellow Commoner, Townsend, subscribed £100. Equally generous as Walpole was Lord Godolphin, who also contributed £500. The College could have done with more of these noble and wealthy alumni, as there were at Trinity or John's. The subscribers list contains 59 names. Some are Fellows, giving small amounts. The Provost did better, with £250. But over 95% of the remainder were Vicars or Rectors (or the occasional bishop), who were former Fellows. This shows that the overwhelming make-up of the college was still clergy aiming at clerical livings, and there was not enough of them with their five, ten, or even twenty guineas to buy even the hundreds of thousands of bricks required for Gibbs, let alone its Portland Stone exterior. The subscribers list as a whole reached £4,655.

With the earlier money and the sale of timber, the College managed to provide about £11,000 in all. But it needed more like £20,000 to complete the job and the accounts move ominously from domestic details such as paying for carriage of bricks, guarding the well on Sunday or providing oil and soap for the crane, to taking out loans and paying workmen on account. The unprecedented expedient was tried of making Fellows pay rent for the rooms and the debt was not mainly paid off until 1758, using a legacy from John Hungerford and by selling the College bells, and not finally extinguished until 1768.

When an appeal for the Chapel was made in 1982 (again mainly to alumni), the College said (in its *Annual Report*) "this is the first major Appeal in the College's history." This was wrong; the first major appeal was in the 1720s. Even for Gibbs, it only covered a quarter of the job and the Gibbs Building as we know it today was only meant to be the side building in a completed court, with a grander building forming a hall on the south side and another accommodation block, exactly matching the current building, along King's Parade. Gibbs was not the first architect for the scheme. Provost Adams had consulted Wren and plans were drawn up by his pupil Hawksmoor under Wren's eye. Wooden models were made to present the plan to potential donors. (They may still be seen in the College library.) Hawksmoor went for a court much as in Gibbs' later plan, with the hall on the south side and two matching accommodation blocks east and west, but he also wanted to recreate the Founder's proposed cloister on where now the back lawn sits. Provost Adams beat him down, and with Provost Snape it was pared further as Gibbs was instead chosen as architect. (This was possibly on party grounds; Gibbs was a Tory rather than a Whig architect.) Only a third of his scheme was constructed and it was stripped of its intended statues and ornamentation; even so, the College went badly into debt before it was finished. Also, as a new building on a green field site away from the centre of the College, it wasn't even popular with Fellows who, apart from paying rent for the privilege, felt too far from the hall and other amenities of the Old Court.

These disappointments were all in the unknown future when on Lady Day 1723, after the traditional Founder's Day sermon to the University by a member of the society, the University and dignitaries came out of King's College Chapel and moved to the building site to lay the foundation stone. The stone was one that tradition held had been cast aside by the workmen when they had heard of the deposition of the Founder. This at least was the story inscribed lengthily on it in Latin before it was buried to take the heavy load placed on it by Gibbs. Earlier in the Chapel, a special anthem had been sung, composed by the College Organist, Thomas Tudway, already over fifty years in post and with some more to go. Mr Hughes had been paid ten guineas to come up from London to sing in it (together with two guineas expenses, some things never change); one of the former Fellows' solemn subscriptions had already been sung away.

A hundred years later, matters moved more smoothly. This time the College had accumulated enough reserves in advance to pay for what it planned. It held an architectural competition, won by William Wilkins. Wilkins did classical at Downing, but here he matched the Chapel with Tudor gothic, repeating its profusion of carved portcullises and roses. Matching no known exemplar, symmetry led him to place the serving bay in the middle of the side of the hall (rather than, as can be seen at Trinity and John's, at the High Table end). Not following any previous plan, he finished the court with an open screen instead of a further accommodation block (which, as we have just seen, was part of the plan of Hawksmoor and Gibbs as well as of the Founder). However, the tiny size of the College has to be remembered. The twenty or thirty resident members must have rattled around inside the enormous hall. Why so large? Presumably it was thought that King's being a grand college, it had to have an over-large hall to match its over-large chapel. But the Chapel had other functions such as prayers for the dead, whereas the hall was never intended to do more than cater for the living. By contrast, the ample accommodation in Wilkins was not merely for the sake of appearance. Part of the cost was obtained by selling the Old Court to the University and so it was needed as replacement accommodation; Wilkins marks the point when not only was the Founder's planned court finally completed after nearly four hundred years but also when King's lost everything that had formed its heart throughout that time.

Wilkins also extended the College westwards towards the river by building a new library and, beyond that, a new Provost's Lodge. The library had started in a small way in the Old Court but Provost Goad had made it serious in the sixteenth century by moving it to the Chapel. For the next century and a half, it occupied the several connected side chapels that now form the vestry, where some of the old bookcases can still be seen. (Others were moved after the construction of the new library to the Provost's Study in the new Provost's Lodge, where they still furnish the room.) The old Provost's Lodge (which had, with other buildings, extended from the east end of the Chapel to about the present front gate) was destroyed and put down to grass; buildings may be changed into grass but they didn't anticipate the modern planning regime that prevents changing grass into buildings. Beside the grass Wilkins built a folly, that is a building without function which was expensive to build and is expensive to maintain. Today, on Cambridge's main street, this space would have been shops and accommodation. Before, as we saw, it was to be accommodation. But what the College got instead was simply a screen. With the screen and the associated demolition of the medieval Provost's Lodge, after Wilkins it was all holes and grass, as if to show that King's was too rich to be concerned with anything other than aesthetic statement.

The aesthetes worried about Gibbs; it did not fit with its flanking gothic structures. So the College formally empowered the Provost to negotiate with Wilkins to gothicise Gibbs. If this had been carried through on Wilkins' plan, Gibbs would have been clothed with spikes and oriels (somewhat like the contemporary operations on the Brighton Pavilion which also encloses a well-mannered eighteenth century house inside its oriental splendour). It would have been joined to the hall range to close the court, where Gibbs had intentionally left his building apart from the Chapel because of its different style and also to create a fire break. However the College did not have the money to complete this additional ornamental project and so the aesthetes and their successors have had to be satisfied with Gibbs as designed by Gibbs.

Wilkins' Building was not in the same way as a century before preceded by a Chapel sermon and a formally placed foundation stone. But the Founder's Day sermon before the University the year it was completed was about the new buildings. It was given by Charles Simeon, who had at one time or another been Bursar, Vice Provost, and Dean. As part of the new building project, the present bridge across the river was built and, at Simeon's urging and partly paid for by him personally, it was moved from its former position facing the centre of the College. (The old causeway to it across Scholar's Piece was gathered into the mounds that still rise from its middle.)

From his position in King's, Simeon was, as Thomas Macaulay remarked, more influential religiously than any bishop or archbishop. The University and College supplied clergy for the Church of England but provided no training for this particular purpose. Simeon set himself to fill the gap with weekly tea time discussions and sermon classes in his rooms above the arch of the Gibbs Building with their large, semi-circular, windows. He was training Evangelical Anglicans and the first Evangelical Archbishop of Canterbury, John Bird Sumner, was a Scholar and Fellow during Simeon's time. The aim was to keep some of the fresh Evangelical fervour inside the Established Church, refreshing it, rather than it being monopolised by the Nonconformists. (Otherwise, as Simeon put it, he beat the trees and the dissenters took the fruit.) As an Evangelical, Simeon was based not in the choral singing Chapel but in his Gibbs' rooms and Holy Trinity, the local church of which he was Vicar. Yet the Chapel, which he had to attend as an undergraduate, was where he was converted and he was also buried there under the initials 'CS' in the centre of the antechapel crossing between the porches.

His funeral was one of the great Cambridge events and fittingly closes this chapter on Old Corruption. Etonian, Kingsman, wealthy, a strong supporter of good causes, he died in his Gibbs rooms on 13 November 1836, just as the bells of Great St Mary's were tolling for the University Sermon that he had been appointed to preach. His funeral was held in Chapel on the following Saturday.

Saturday morning was a busy market day for the town and a time for undergraduate lectures. Yet the shops were closed, the market was deserted, and the colleges cancelled their lectures. People in the streets wore mourning and many, town and gown alike, converged on King's for Simeon's last ceremony. The townspeople ineligible for admission massed against the railing that then topped the wall along King's Parade and the members of Simeon's congregation at Holy Trinity were admitted to the antechapel. Meanwhile the members of the University, in their black academic dress with added black ribbons and scarves of mourning, assembled in the new College hall while the members of King's combined in the new Combination Room next to it in the same building. Something like 1500 people emerged to process with the coffin round the newly completed Front Court: a verger, the choristers in their surplices, the conduct, the Scholars, the Fellows, the Provost, Simeon in his coffin accompanied by eight senior Fellows, the chief family mourner, eight heads of other Cambridge colleges, and then the professors, MAs, BAs, and undergraduates in proper order.

The antechapel when they entered was filled with townspeople, very many of them women, sighing and crying, all dressed in deep mourning. The University men passed through to the east end where the service was read by the Provost and the choristers sang. For the final part of the ceremony, the coffin was taken back to the antechapel and the Provost read most impressively before Simeon was lowered into the vault beneath and the 'Dead March in Saul' was performed with grand thunders on the organ.

CHAPTER SIX

THE NEW KING'S

This chapter takes the story from the 1850s to the 1950s; or, to put it more pedantically, from the election of Provost Okes in 1850 to the election of Provost Annan in 1956. During this period, the College moved from the cocooned corrupt club described in the last chapter to a vibrant intellectual community open to all comers. It started tiny, rattling round inside its new buildings; it ended as a normal sized college, much more in balance with its continuing imposing presence. It started as a college unworried by the University examination results since it did not bother taking them. It ended equally unworried, but now because it was consistently rated best in the University. It is the period when in many people's opinion the College reaches its zenith; it is the period of M R James, E M Forster, Turing and Keynes. We see in this chapter King's totally, almost unrecognisably, transformed, yet continuing to be a college whose peculiarity can be partially explained by its peculiar history.

However strange in retrospect, things were done in the eighteenth century just because that was how things were always done. By the 1850s, when this chapter starts, they had ceased to seem appropriate. Reform and Rationality were in the air and even the established church for which Cambridge was the seminary had to respond.

We can catch the flavour of the pressure to reform in the Church from two partly satirical novels written in this decade. George Eliot's first work, *Scenes of Clerical Life*, starts with its narrator musing about "the well regulated mind, which unintermittingly rejoices in the New Police, the Tithe Commutation Act, the penny post, and all guarantees of human advancement, and has no moments when conservative-reforming intellect takes a nap, while the imagination does a little Toryism by the sly, revelling in regret that the dear, old, brown, crumbling, picturesque inefficiency is everywhere giving place to spick-and-span new-painted, new-varnished efficiency." (Incidentally, the work's central character was an evangelical clergyman "whose Christian experiences ... had been consolidated at Cambridge under the influence of Mr. Simeon.") More familiar is Trollope's *The Warden* where the Wardenship, a place acquired through the right contacts and requiring little work in exchange for its stipend, comes under pressure to be reformed into a position for which a rationally chosen occupant is required to fulfil his rationally specified function to justify his pay.

In this contest, King's Fellowships were worse than Trollope's unreformed Wardenship and slept with George Eliot's unreformed nap; it was "picturesque inefficiency". A Fellowship gave an unmarried man a salary for life as well as rooms and commons in College and was acquired because someone had the right contacts at the age of thirteen. There were no serious subsequent examinations and after becoming a Fellow there was no required work of any kind. The College had, in Cambridge terms, a large income and it spent it on a few well favoured people. It followed the Founder's plan of life support for Etonians, but the Founder had planned for them to be closeted in the College, singing daily in Chapel and following for decades an extended course of study. By contrast, the considerable majority of Fellows now lived and worked elsewhere, using their Fellowship stipend to supplement their other earnings and only coming once a term to College meetings to prevent any upset of their gravy train. Some, the minority, still lived in College. But they went nowhere near the Chapel and were academically idle; they did not teach and they did not research. Similarly for the undergraduates: they were few in number, supported by the College, unperturbed by University examinations, and could look forward to automatically securing Fellowships. We saw in the last chapter that King's had 30 residents when Trinity, with roughly similar resources, had 351. In this new reforming age, the question naturally arose of whether the College's considerable wealth was being devoted to the right (or, indeed, even the Founder's) purposes.

The eventual answer was to create what was called The New King's. Fellowships ceased to be given automatically but became competitive and could not be held beyond six years without working for the College. Students were entered for University examinations for which they were now taught by College Fellows. Most importantly, the College opened out and expanded its student population so that it no longer came from a single school. Some of this was devised by the College itself in many meetings considering the Statutes. But the chief moving force was external pressure. Just as centuries before the government had been concerned to keep Cambridge in the right religious groove, now after a century and a half of neglect it returned, this time to eliminate abuses. As George Eliot's remark implies, it was Whig (later called Liberal) pressure, tidying up sleeping Toryism. Bishoprics, the army, the civil service, and Trollope's fictional Wardenship were examined and reformed. For Cambridge, Royal Commissions were first created to examine and report. Then Acts of Parliament were passed giving Commissioners powers to produce new statutes. This happened in two waves of reform. The first Commission was in the 1850s and resulted in the 1861 Statutes for King's, the first new set since the Founder's. Then a second wave produced the 1882 Statutes, which effectively governed the College through the rest of this chapter.

The 1850 Commissioners reported that they had "experienced great difficulties" with "the peculiar circumstances of the Foundation of King's College." But they did not have that much difficulty in showing how many of the Founder's Statutes the College had ceased to observe, concluding that "scarcely any part remains in force but what is dependent upon the relative rights of the various members of the body, or upon its union with the sister foundation of Eton." In these circumstances, breaking the Eton monopoly might have been the natural conclusion. But even the Commissioners did not dare go that far, wondering merely whether Fellowships might not also be open to Etonians from other colleges. It was the College itself that made the decisive move, using the 1861 Statutes to open up the student body to non-Etonians and establishing Open Scholarships to match the Eton Scholarships.

The 1861 Statutes fundamentally changed the student body and the 1882 Statutes fundamentally changed the Fellowship. Nathaniel Wedd, who later became a Fellow himself, arrived in 1883, a year after the second set of new Statutes. In his memoir of this year he says that "in 1883 King's was a very young college". In one way, for a college over four centuries old, this was absurd. In another way, it is completely correct. This was a new King's, new in the formation of its Fellowship and completely changed in its student body. Twenty-one new students started with Wedd as compared to the four or so annually admitted in the first part of the century. There were students from local grammar schools and London day schools, a Japanese and a Canadian, as well as from leading public schools. Students in addition to the Eton Scholars had been admitted in the sixteenth and the seventeenth century before the College withdrew completely into its Etonian core. Now they came again and soon formed the great majority, as had never happened before. The first were admitted in 1865 and, with Fellowships now open to all students, the first ever Fellow not from Eton was elected in 1873. In the same year, the first Open Scholars were admitted. Soon the College ran a single competitive entrance examination at Cambridge (replacing the Posers going to Eton) to award Scholarships to both Etonians and others, providing significant financial support. By the time Wedd arrived from the City of London School as one of these

Open Scholars, the new system was firmly in place with a recently appointed cadre of Teaching Fellows, which in due course he joined.

These teachers were controlled by a Tutor, the benevolent and efficient George Prothero, who lived with his recently married wife at the King's Parade end of King's Lane. For by the new 1882 Statutes Fellows no longer were required to resign on marriage and in the case of the Senior Tutor this meant the wife coming into College rather than the Fellow departing to the suburbs. (Prothero was the second Fellow to marry; the first left for the hills of Shelford.) "We all knew," Wedd wrote, "that Prothero was a friend." Following Wedd's first term in Prothero's diary, we find the new Scholars admitted and then later taken by the Tutor to the Senate House to be matriculated. By the start of November Prothero noted that he had "worked off" the freshmen and was engaged in selling tickets for *The Birds*, the Greek play in which King's was central. He gave his lectures for the University on the seventeenth century and at the end of term there was the Annual Congregation which "began with tragedy" with one of the two Deans attempting "impeachment of Bursars", which in turn meant that he was voted out as Dean. Prothero solaced himself that evening by seeing *The Birds;* good music, fair acting, "but a comedy won't do 2000 years after." This is new King's, and in certain elements it is starting to be recognisable.

Moving to the end of that academic year, we find in Prothero's diary for June the CUMS concert (Brahms Requiem; Beethoven Seventh); the College concert; marking the University honours examinations (then, as now, called the 'Tripos'); the prizes meeting of College Council; and the results in the Classics and the Maths Tripos. The conscientious Tutor notes six Classics firsts and three Wranglers, "splendid", and three days later he takes twenty men to the Senate House to be presented for their BA degrees before having the new Professor of Ecclesiastical History to lunch. This is a still familiar rhythm (with only a slight adjustment of Degree Day lunch). So it is worth cutting further into it to see how it was achieved. M R James, ghost story writer and later Provost, came to King's in the year before Wedd. Monty James was the kind of person who could have come at any time since the foundation: King's Scholar at Eton (like his father), he moved on to being Scholar and Fellow of King's (like his father). But, as he points out himself in his own memoir, he was the only Etonian in his year in an entry of fifteen. In fact, this was an unusual year. It was unusually small and, more importantly, unusually thin on Scholars coming from the College at Eton. In the year before James there were four and the year after (Wedd's year) there were also four. These numbers are very like the numbers at the start of the century; the Eton Scholars had not disappeared but had simply been swamped.

In Wedd's year, the four Eton Scholars were matched by four Open Scholars. Every one of these eight Entrance Scholars subsequently went on to achieve a First Class in Tripos (6 Classics, one Natural Sciences, one Law). The other 15 only achieved one First between them, as well as 5 Seconds, 5 Thirds, and 2 not taking the Tripos. So although the traditional Etonian entry might have been swamped, it still contributed significantly to the results. The four Eton Scholars in the year before James all got Firsts, as did James himself. The men whose results Prothero saluted as splendid, in both Classics and Mathematics, contained several Eton Scholars. This pattern persists through the period covered in this chapter. The Entrance Scholars are throughout a distinctive intellectual elite with noticeably better results, and a sizeable proportion of the Entrance Scholars are Eton Scholars.

Another reason why Wedd would not have been accepted earlier was his religion, or lack of it. Until the 1882 Statutes every Fellow of King's had to swear that he was "a bona fide member of the Church of England" before being admitted to his Fellowship. When this chapter starts, all students were required to be communicating members of the Anglican Church (with a termly communion in Chapel to check that everyone was signed up) and all Fellows were required to become priests after a certain interval (although not all did); the normal career pattern was to move from a Fellowship to being a Vicar or Rector in one of the College's carefully acquired livings. Then, after the 1871 Test Act, students entered with other religions and Fellows no longer needed to resign (as they did at other colleges, but not at King's) because they acquired conscientious scruples about the 39 Articles that set out the official doctrine of the Church of England.

The entry of the dissenters was particularly important at King's. It was overwhelmingly public school in its intake (like the other colleges) but it opened itself up to new schools just at the point new religions were allowed. The other colleges had their established links with the leading Anglican schools and so it was natural for King's to draw from dissenting academies that only now could send their boys to Cambridge. So a considerable number of Quakers came to King's as well as Methodists. Among the latter was John Clapham (who arrived in 1892), later Senior Tutor, University Professor, and President of the British Academy. Indeed if we look at the people who ran King's between the wars, and so had been undergraduates before the First World War, we find that many of them (such as Sheppard, Keynes, and Clapham) had dissenting backgrounds. The then Professor of Ancient History, Frank Adcock, would seem to be the epitome of an establishment figure: bachelor don, conservative tastes, intelligence officer in the War. Yet just as Sir John Clapham was the son of a Methodist Manchester silversmith, Sir Frank Adcock was the son of a Methodist Leicester elementary schoolteacher. He came from a family with no previous university connection, went to the local grammar school, and retained a trace of his local accent.

Adcock, Wedd, and Clapham are good examples of Open Scholars from different backgrounds, matching the Eton Scholars and achieving equally good results. They all went into the melting pot. But in the 1880s the new entry led to a nearly calamitous conflict in the College, which persisted in later and less serious cultural divisions. As E M Forster (who arrived in 1897) put it, it was the division between the exclusive and the excluded. Charles Tennyson (who arrived two years later) revised this by dividing the excluded into those that wanted to be included and those that did not. It was the latter that were the irritatingly important part of what gave King's its special texture. Wedd said that the great majority of his year "found ourselves quickly placed on the black list, and would not have it otherwise." Tennyson claims that such desired exclusion generated individuality and supplied new life to the University; Wedd similarly claimed that it led them to question received values so that they "called the bluff of good form". Not then particularly political, this strand of wilful difference leads to the later membership of the Fabian Society by King's undergraduates (like Rupert Brooke and Hugh Dalton, who both arrived in 1906 with impeccable establishment backgrounds) and so to the College's left-leaning tradition.

Part of this distinction was as superficial as dress and also divided the dons. It was a manifestation of how a traditional college, all of whose members came from a common culture, struggled to accommodate itself to a profound change in its composition. All the newly appointed teachers came from Old King's and all had been Scholars of the College after being King's Scholars at Eton. They wanted the new reformed King's to work, unlike Grant the Bursar who was a straightforward reactionary. But this could cause them problems. The most interesting case was the Junior Tutor, Arthur Augustus Tilley. Tilley believed in the new order but was offended by the dress, behaviour, and taste of many whose entry the new order permitted. It was because of him that the creative conflict came to a nasty head in 1889. The Junior Tutor suggested to the exquisites that they might dump one of the offensives in the Front Court fountain and when this had happened with the unpleasant effect of the man becoming so ill that he had to leave, the undergraduates revolted against Prothero's Assistant Tutor. Tilley had to resign and was moved sideways, first into a Classics Lectureship and then into being the Modern Languages Lecturer, creating the subject at King's. Monty James, hitherto very much a best set person, restored calm by calling all the undergraduates together and getting the two sides to agree to respect each other.

Modern Languages was one of the new Triposes created in later nineteenth century Cambridge. Until the mid-century there were only Mathematics and Classics and even in the 1880s these were still dominant, in King's as elsewhere. Moral Sciences and Natural Sciences were created in the 1850s; Moral Sciences never really took off but Natural Sciences advanced slowly, even though the College did not have a Fellow to teach the subject until 1895. The one new Tripos in which King's did specialise was History and throughout the period covered by this chapter King's was very much a Classics and History college. In the 1880s most of the teaching dons taught Classics but History was supported by the accidental near simultaneous acquisition of Prothero and Oscar Browning, who both had been teaching Classics at Eton. Prothero was lured back to help construct the new King's and Browning decided to return after being sacked by Eton for having been too friendly with the boys. With their very different temperaments and in their very different ways, they between them created a History School.

Oscar Browning (universally known as 'OB') was the stuff and conscious creator of legends. A massive egomaniac for whom the very worst eventuality was to be ignored, even posthumously he makes it difficult. Browning thought that the transformation of King's could be dated back to 1856 (as it happens, the year that he came). Like him or loathe him (and he easily encouraged either reaction) he assisted the College's culture wars as a promoter of bad form. (Apart from anything else, after his treatment by the Headmaster he had an unsurprising antagonism to Eton.) He opened up new areas, made undergraduates believe in themselves, and encouraged them to study Mozart and Dante before either became fashionable. And, as an inexhaustible subject of undergraduate anecdotes, he kept the College cheerful.

In fact, as well as the absurd stream of half way hilarious happenings, there is much about Browning that explains the advent and composition of the new King's. To start with, there is not just society but societies; the College was full of discussion groups.

Browning's was the Political Society, which was initially open by invitation to Trinity and King's undergraduates. Papers were read and comments made in an order determined by lot. Although a History society, its name indicated Browning's belief that the new History Tripos was to be an instrument of political education (and the History of Political Thought, from the start a prominent part of the Tripos, was lectured on in the University by both Prothero and Browning). The format was similar to that most famous Cambridge secret society, the Apostles, and Browning as an Apostle was a close friend of Trinity Apostles, in particular Henry Sidgwick and Henry Jackson. These were the men who reformed college teaching, particularly in Classics and History. (It has often been observed how supposed immemorial practices are in fact an invention of the late nineteenth century; this includes Cambridge's sacred supervision system.)

At Eton, Browning had been a pupil of William Johnson, Assistant Master and King's Fellow. As indeed almost all the Assistant Masters were. If the inaccurate short story about how King's awoke from its slumbers and became great is that it got rid of Eton, the somewhat more accurate story of how Eton did likewise is that it got rid of King's. Johnson, a repressed homosexual like Browning, was similarly sacked by the same Headmaster for being too friendly with the boys. What he particularly promoted was the wide ranging intellectual development of his pupils through a tutorial system and it was this Etonian custom come to Cambridge that led to the new college teaching system in King's and Trinity. Unlike Browning, Johnson did not come back to King's after being sacked (but instead changed his name to Cory). However, earlier, as a member of King's Governing Body committee elected in the 1850s to consider reform, he was a strong supporter and influential creator of the new King's.

Johnson worked closely in developing the idea of the new college with Henry Bradshaw, a resident Fellow with great moral authority. Bradshaw also encouraged undergraduates, particularly those that felt awkward or different. His rooms were open to students dropping in; Browning later had a rumbustious party every Sunday evening on A staircase, and Monty James was so used to undergraduates dropping in that when he became Provost he removed the lock from a door to give them free access. Apart from this general sociability, there were two specific things that were felt by every generation covered by this chapter to be importantly distinctive about King's. Firstly, there were close connections between Fellows and students, so that students acquired things from the dons more as they might from older brothers rather than from distant and patriarchal figures. Secondly, what they picked up was a wider interest, even inside their subject, than simply trying to do well in examinations. Both were easier to achieve when everyone came from the same house of the same school. But the point of the New King's is that a sufficient nucleus of Fellows managed to carry them forward with the broader intake. These students in turn as Fellows transmitted it to the next generation, and so on.

Even if the dons didn't want the students restricted by examinations, the evolution of examinations at Cambridge is importantly explanatory. The University shook itself from its profound eighteenth century slumber when it introduced competitive examinations. It started with the Maths Tripos and the important scientists of early nineteenth century Cambridge were men who had started their careers by coming top of the Maths Tripos. When Classics joined Maths, it was initially only available to people who were classed in Maths. (Hence the original, or true, meaning of 'Double First', which was a First in both of these subjects.) None of this affected King's whose students took their degrees upon request and without any examination. But in the 1850s, when this chapter starts, two things happened. People could take the Classics Tripos without also taking Maths and King's decided to take University examinations. The latter change was long overdue. Fellows had campaigned for it; pamphlets were written; and the Visitor approached. But it had the implacable opposition of the Provost, Thackeray, at a time when Provosts wielded a veto. When Thackeray died, the Visitor discussed the matter with the new

Provost, Richard Okes, and Okes arrived determined to make the change, which happened in 1851.

Well before the College opened out beyond Eton, therefore, its students were doing the Tripos. Then, after it opened up, it was decided that every student should take a Tripos examination, unless there were good reasons otherwise. Keeping King's an honour college in this way gave it a distinctive identity and was important to its self-image. Each college had some 'reading men' who worked and took the Tripos while the others (at this point the majority) played and passed out in 'the Poll' (from *hoi polloi*, the people). The poll men paid an annual £10 fee, got some college instruction, and took a general examination before getting their degree. The Tripos men engaged their own coaches at £60 annually and entered the formidable competition of the Maths and Classics Triposes. Everyone's ranking was published, so the aim was to be best of the year (the Senior Wrangler or Senior Classic) or, failing that, to come very high up the order. The leading coaches took the best men and the porters of the leading colleges bet on their runners who they could see daily coming through their Lodges as an alternative to the runners at Newmarket.

This was the system that the College joined, gaining many Senior Classics, although in the something over fifty years until the rankings were no longer published it only managed one Senior Wrangler, the same as Newnham (where, since ladies were not allowed degrees, she was simply "above the Senior Wrangler"). The coaches were teaching the tricks of Tripos; that was, after all, why they were expensively hired. So the challenge in bringing serious teaching back into the colleges was to match the results of the coaches while also showing that there was more to the subject, and indeed life, than the tricks of the Tripos. This was managed in Classics and more easily achieved in History, where the new Tripos had not the same embedded external competition.

With more and different students produced by the initial reform, the College created the position of Tutor. The first was William

Ralph Churton of Browning's year (1856), who became both Tutor and Dean in 1865. After two years, he rather gladly relinquished the tutorial part of his responsibilities and so Augustus Austen Leigh was brought back to be Tutor. He served from 1868 until 1881, when he handed over to Prothero. It was Austen Leigh who first employed the new cadre of teachers and tirelessly built up the new King's. He was afterwards Vice Provost (effectively acting as Provost for the aging Okes) and then Provost from 1889 to 1905. With an annual admission in single figures when he started, it had reached about fifty a year by the time he died as Provost. This greatly expanded body had to be taught and housed in a college designed since its foundation for seventy Scholars and Fellows.

The Provost lost his veto in the first Statutory reforms and the final say in matters of government was in the hands of the Fellowship as a whole. Even after the new teaching Fellows had been appointed, the majority of Fellows were not resident; only 18 of the 47 Fellows were resident in 1883 and earlier the proportion was even smaller. A special carriage was attached to the London train to bring non-residents to Governing Body meetings. Every Fellow drew money from his Fellowship and somehow a majority had to be persuaded of the merits of diverting money from Fellowships. Reform meant Open Scholarships to match the Eton Scholarships, paid for by central College funds. A new cadre of teaching Fellows meant paying for College Lecturers. The Tutor (and also the Junior Tutor when it was decided, as at the time of Tilley, to have an assistant) meant further stipends. The plan was to reduce the Fellowship to 46 and have 24 Eton Scholars and 24 Open Scholars. (The shadow of the sacred seventy persists in the sum of 46 Fellows and 24 Eton Scholars.) But the plan was hit by unexpected internal and external accidents, which delayed its achievement.

When the plan was formulated, the College was at its most prosperous and naturally assumed that this would continue. Money came from agricultural rents and what was not foreseen was a prolonged and serious agricultural depression. The surplus income divided between the Fellows, known as the Dividend, which was £260 per Fellow in the 1860s, had fallen to £80 by the start of the next century. A dissident non-resident Fellow, not seeing why his income should be cut to pay scholarships for people not from his old school, appealed to the Visitor. The Visitor, with no inkling of the forthcoming collapse in rents, made an utterly bizarre judgement securing an increased income to all existing Fellows. This would have been disastrous even for maintaining the old system, let alone introducing the new one, and was only circumvented by every Fellow apart from the dissident agreeing not to take the awarded additional income. So the dissident carried on with his legal practice, happily drawing his unearned additional income, while the College painfully wondered how to provide money for scholarships and buildings.

For just when the College was seriously squeezed was when it had to build to accommodate the expanded student body. First it extended south along King's Parade, with a building of the leading Victorian architect, George Gilbert Scott. The next step in that direction was the Bull Hotel, belonging to St Catharine's. A price was agreed but purchase was prevented by the Copyholder Commissioners. It may be surprising, particularly with respect to the nineteenth century, that a purchase between a willing buyer and a willing seller could be prevented. But the Commissioners, checking that fair prices were being paid, judged that King's, with its additional building options, was offering too much whereas St Catharine's, with no alternative building site, was accepting too little; clearly in these circumstances no amount of renegotiation would satisfy them. So the next step would be to buy St Catharine's although, obviously, it was never put in such terms. The plan, passed by both colleges' governing bodies and with all details agreed by a joint committee, was to unite the two colleges. The combined college was to be familiarly called 'King's and St Katherine's' with the current King's Provost as its first Provost. However, with the deal apparently securely sewn up, the few Fellows of St Catharine's took fright and it unravelled.

Another alternative was to replace the Wilkins Screen along King's Parade with accommodation, as had always been intended until Wilkins got to work. It may seem untouchable to us today, with its framing of the famous chapel from which it quotes. Yet a majority of Fellows was in favour of its removal and a book written by a Fellow in 1867 called it a "masterpiece of extravagance and bad taste"; an "error" to be rectified by removal. A competition was held for which three leading architects (Scott, Street, and Burges) made submissions. Austen Leigh himself was not so sure: such a prominent site demanded an expensive building and it would be cheaper to find the accommodation somewhere further south. The majority faded and the tenements on the far side of King's Lane were fitted up as student accommodation before Chetwynd Court was completed with a lecture room and accommodation facing Scott's Building across the Court.

We now reach the point when Wedd arrived; this is the college to which he came with the newly married Senior Tutor living besides the students in King's Lane. The new lecture room was inaugurated with a lecture on Whichcote (the Provost intruded by the Parliamentarians) given by Brooke Foss Westcott. One provision of the new Statutes was that King's should have four Professorial Fellows and Westcott, later Bishop of Durham, was the first to be elected. The Professorial Fellowships had a very positive influence on King's, bringing people in from outside, connecting it with the newly research aware University, and introducing new subjects.

The 1882 Statutes therefore opened up the Fellowship just as the 1861 Statutes had opened up the student body. With entry to the Fellowship no longer automatic, a strict competition was devised, analogous to the stiff student competition for entrance scholarships. Every year at the Annual Congregation the Electors to Fellowships were themselves elected. Every year in March they elected members of the College to prize Fellowships. Soon they decided to do this mainly by dissertation rather than relying on Tripos results with the result that non-Tripos subjects were occasionally considered and men elected who had not done particularly well in Tripos; in this way Edward Dent was the first Music Fellow in Cambridge and Rupert Brooke was elected in English Literature. These March elections lasted longer than the period covered in this chapter and produced many of the best known King's Fellows. It was this competition that added to the Fellowship Keynes, Sheppard, Clapham, and Turing (but not E M Forster, who was elected to a different kind of Fellowship in 1927). They had it as a prize for six years, after which they only continued on the Fellowship if they had a College position such as Dean, Bursar, or Lecturer.

The Fellowship did not expand significantly until after the Second World War, staying somewhere near the 48 to which the reformers had reduced it. But the College continually had to expand its accommodation to match the expanding student body. The next chance came when Provost Okes died in 1889 and Austen Leigh succeeded. The river end of the Provost's Garden was seized and Bodley's built. Then, in turn, when Austen Leigh died, some of the most eastern parts of the Provost's territory could be liberated and, by moving King's Lane southwards, Webb's Building was constructed and Webb's Court created; marking Monty James' time as Provost, his initials can be seen carved on the inside gate tower.

In King's, unlike other larger colleges, a single alphabetical sequence has always sufficed to identify the staircases. It is worth following this sequence to understand King's in the period that we have now reached, the golden period before the Great War. The letters then painted or carved mainly still exist and all of A to D can still be seen painted on the four entrances to Wilkins, even if today we only think of A as a staircase. B and C are the passages on each side of the hall; B then also led to accommodation and C led to the SCR. Staircase D, like A, was a nest of dons. The next four letters (E to H) still identify the staircases of Gibbs, although it was then a wholly residential building that contained many undergraduates as well as dons. For these classicists, I and J were the same letter. So J is next, still painted at the bottom of the elaborate external spiral staircase of Scott's building in Chetwynd Court. It shows that Scott's was then a completely separate building, with its own entrance and accommodation on every floor on each side of the staircase. Crossing Chetwynd Court, we would have found K and L, two accommodation staircases in the lecture block, before jumping to the far side of King's Lane to find M and N, the undergraduate accommodation constructed from the old tenements. After that the alphabet is familiar again from O to W, with O to R in Webb's and S to W in Bodley's. No X, however, for the northern half closure of this court did not exist before the First World War. When Forster in his Cambridge novel *The Longest Journey* imagines them speaking about the cow, the view from Forster's rooms in Bodley's to the cows on Scholar's Piece was through a dignified line of elms rather than round the corner of X staircase.

Even this much building managed only to house about half of this greatly expanded college; the other undergraduates lived in lodgings. The separation between Scholars and pensioners was not only in results but extended to accommodation. Scholars lived all three years in College; this was particularly pronounced in the first year where the new Scholars lived together in King's while nearly all the rest lived out. When Maynard Keynes arrived in 1902, he came to the converted tenements in King's Lane (staircases M and N). The same was the case for Scholars throughout this chapter and until they were demolished in the 1960s (whereupon the last Scholars took away the staircase sign and still meet as 'The M Club'). Such Scholars naturally combined and some of Keynes' best initial friends were those with him in the Lane. Or, as it was usually called, the Drain, after the insalubrious underground passage by which it was reached from the rest of the College, and Keynes left his legacy to demolish the Drain.

Keynes was reading Maths, but he fitted naturally with Charles Fay, History Open Scholar and Robin Furness, Classics Open Scholar and expert in erotica. Then Keynes, like John Sheppard two years before him, became an Apostle, President of the Union, member of many discussion societies, or anything but studying his subject (although he did in the end manage 12th Wrangler, not that far behind William Page, who entered with him as an Open Scholar from a local grammar school and worked solidly throughout; these were the only two Kingsmen in a list of 77.) The (once again sole) Tutor responsible for this gallery was W H Macaulay. Somewhat surprisingly for someone presiding over this golden pre-war generation, Macaulay was an Engineer. He had previously been Second Bursar and electrified the College after building Bodley's; Keynes posthumously thought that he was "the best Home Bursar and best Tutor that recent generations have known."

When the Great War came twelve years after their arrival at King's, most of these Scholars were not combatants but, like Keynes himself, served otherwise. It was the younger men who fought and died in the largest numbers. Current and prospective undergraduates left to join the army and the effect was devastating on the College. In the summer of 1914, when the war started, 170 students were expected in the coming term. In fact 64 arrived. After Easter it was 31 and after that it was only the unfit and the foreigners; in October 1916, 1917, and 1918 the total numbers of undergraduates were 22, 17, and 16. The Fellows departed to serve in offices or trenches; four, most famously Rupert Brooke, perished in the cause. The cricket field shared with Clare behind the Fellows Garden was turned into a large hospital for wounded men, run by two medical Fellows of King's. The nurses were boarded in the empty College rooms; by 1914 they had already taken over Bodley's, later they also occupied Chetwynd Court with a common room in Gibbs. The life went out of not only the men but also the College and Monty Rhodes James, who served for two years as University Vice Chancellor at the start of this unfortunate period, presided as Provost over a ghost. In 1918 he eagerly escaped to Eton, becoming the only person to be Provost of both of King Henry's twin foundations.

Similarly, earlier in 1918, Eric Milner-White returned to his old haunts; chaplain in the forces, something went wrong with the army and the College also wished to make him Dean. (The stories about the army vary; one is that with all the officers killed, he improperly replaced them as a combatant.) Milner was a dominating Dean until in 1941 he left to be Dean of York. His immediate task was to remember the sacrifice; 174 (23%) of the 774 who served had lost their lives. The south eastern side chapel (Provost Argentein's chantry) was turned into a memorial chapel with the stone wall facing the glass covered with the names of the dead. Just as when they were in the Drain, the Scholars are separated even in the record of their final sacrifice. The order is: Fellows, Scholars, others (and for anyone who is puzzled, the order inside each category is by date of admission rather than being alphabetical; it is strictly hierarchical). The problem of the man who had been killed fighting for the wrong side was solved by carving his name on an orthogonal wall.

Milner-White was an expert in glass and installed or reordered the glass in both this and the other side chapels. He put his own personal mark on the glass in the war memorial chapel with the arms of Harrow (his school), King's, and the War Chaplaincy; underneath in Latin is a quotation from the Psalms thanking the Lord for covering his head in time of battle. The sunlit colours of Milner's glass crawl over the names of the fallen and I had a fantasy that the rich red robes of the kings above his personal memorial were so placed that on the eleventh hour of the eleventh day of the eleventh month the sun would throw warm gules on fair Fitzgerald's name; Gerald Fitzgerald, fellow Harrovian, having been Milner's special friend. However, unfortunately, it doesn't quite work (even if we allow for the equation of time, then at a maximum).

The other memorial that Milner instituted was the Christmas Eve service, first held in 1918, less than two months after the end of the war. The Choir had greatly improved since A H ('Daddy') Mann became Organist in 1876 and in the same decade the boarding school built for the choristers and Choral Scholars elected to replace lay clerks. It had always sung at Christmas and Monty James annually had a party staying in the Provost's Lodge and telling ghost stories. But Milner started (although he did not invent) the Festival of Nine Lessons and Carols, with his eloquent bidding prayer remembering those "who rejoice with us, but upon another shore and in a greater light"; back once again in College, the living were haunted by missing faces.

With Milner-White holding the Chapel, Keynes ascended the bursarial ranks (becoming Second Bursar in 1919 and First Bursar in 1924), and Clapham was Tutor until his Professorship in 1929. His successor, Sandy Wollaston, explorer and member of the first British Everest expedition, did not survive long, being shot dead by a student he was trying to help in the Tutor's room on F staircase. He was followed by Donald Beves, who stayed as Tutor until after the Second War, with Keynes continuing as First Bursar, Sheppard (from 1933) Provost, and Clapham brought back to replace Sheppard as Vice Provost. A large number still studied Classics and History; Economics was not as popular as might be expected (this waited until after the next war) and the new subject of English drew in several students although not as many as Modern Languages, nor with particularly good results. With its Bloomsbury connections, King's was identified as the Cambridge centre of evil by the Leavisites and F L Lucas fought back fiercely on behalf of the College. Meanwhile above the Webb's Court gateway in his room decorated by his Bloomsbury friends (with suitably naked men and clothed women) Keynes' seminar argued through the ideas that resulted in his *General Theory* of 1936.

F L Lucas, introduced to teach English, was imported from Trinity. So also was F P Ramsey to teach Maths; although Ramsey died before he was thirty, he made still remembered contributions in Economics, Philosophy, and the Foundations of Mathematics. The 1882 Statutes allowed the election of Fellows from outside in addition to the Professorial Fellows and the College was now starting to make serious use of this provision. An open competition was held in 1923, won by Patrick Blackett, later Nobel Prizewinner in Physics. By the start of the 1930s, four specially funded regular external competitions had been set up that between them covered the academic field.

New Fellowships and more Open Scholarships were possible because of a change in the College's fortunes, chiefly owed to Keynes. He increased income by shifting from agricultural rents to equities as well as increasing capital. Keynes was a builder and in George Kennedy he acquired an architect he trusted. They completed Bodley's Court, built a new Provost's Lodge, and turned accommodation into a new larger SCR. It was done with straight lines, rational and classical in reaction against the pointed gothic twiddles of nineteenth century medievalism. The contrast can be seen in the arcade Kennedy opened up under the library: it is Wilkins pointed on the north side and classical columns on the south. So also the SCR, with its filled in pointed Wilkins window and its new square Kennedy window looking west. (After Keynes let in the light, Milner seized the stone and built yet another altar.)

Wherever Kennedy went, he marked his way with classical columns, such as those that frame the main door to the Provost's Lodge. Just as Wilkins himself had been instructed to gothicise Gibbs, so now Kennedy was instructed to classicise Wilkins. He started with S staircase (where the white 'Kennedy infill' still sits in startling stylistic and colour contrast to the rest of the building run). The plan was to replace yellow pointy Wilkins with something white and chaste, matching Gibbs and such as had been started with S. Unlike earlier building projects, the money was there. However it was defeated on aesthetic grounds at the Governing Body after a speech by a junior Fellow whose greater distance from the Victorians made his generation more inclined to value rather than to destroy neo-gothic architecture.

Keynes had more luck on and across the road. The railings that protected the College from King's Parade were removed and Kennedy replaced them with a wall, consciously intended as a long stone seat for the citizens of Cambridge. Keynes bought property on the far side and created the hostel now known as Spalding. Then, with

Kennedy again as architect and financed largely by himself, he built the Arts Theatre. Internally in the shape of a pentagon, which was also its symbol, it was designed to support five arts: drama, music, opera, ballet, and cinema. It had a gala ballet opening and regular cinema shows. Drama fitted well with the period. The many discussion groups of before the war were largely replaced by play reading groups. Donald Beves was a very talented actor. Dadie Rylands, one of F L Lucas' first pupils, directed many Marlowe Society productions and promoted a superior way of speaking Shakespeare that changed the national style.

And so again to war. Sir Alfred Ewing, former Engineering Professorial Fellow, had been in charge of the Admiralty's code breaking facility in the First World War (Room 40), employing Adcock to assist. With this Second World War, the College again turned to code breaking, Adcock recruited and many Fellows (most famously Alan Turing) worked as code-breakers at Bletchley Park. The College was again invaded, not this time by nurses but by Americans. Queen Mary College was evacuated from London to King's. With the risk of bomb destruction, the Chapel glass was stored in cellars (apart, tellingly, from the west window added in the nineteenth century) and Fellows took turns in fire-watching from the roof. The Christmas Eve service continued on the radio through the war from an unspecified although clearly identifiable location.

Afterwards, another wall of fallen names was carved and the windows slowly replaced. To the great delight of Provost Sheppard (a royalist would-be radical), the King and Queen came to celebrate the restoration and the College kept up the pretence of carrying on much as before. But the undergraduates bulged with a large number of returned, older, and battle-hardened men and even when this bulge had passed through, National Service meant a continuation of more mature students. Keynes died just after the War; it is rather amazing that when he was central in creating the post-war world financial system at Bretton Woods he was still Bursar of King's, worrying about tiny parochial concerns. Ronald Balfour, the young Fellow who had stopped his building and was expected to become Assistant Tutor, was killed right at the war's end.

They, with the other men written on the wall, were missing. But the second slaughter was nothing like as extreme as the first and the College continued for a decade after the war in recognisable continuity with not just before this one but also before the first one. It was musical, artistic, and interested in theatre. It was public school and male. It valued Classics and History. There were sufficient Scholars to enable it to do well, but it aimed not to make a fetish of examinations. It valued difference and character. The Fellowship and student body were bound together by personal ties and the feeling that their college was mildly progressive and so somewhat different from the rest of Cambridge.

CHAPTER SEVEN

STORY'S END

This chapter completes the story, taking the history of the College from the mid-1950s up to the present day. In the last chapter we saw it fundamentally changed; in this chapter it changes even further and faster. Its formal face at the start is captured in a film made of the 1955 Christmas Eve Service. In part this is still fully familiar, with the same readings as at present and even some of the same, somewhat esoteric, carols. But the flickering black and white film also reveals an alien past in which ladies wear hats, men wear suits and ties, and everyone looks at home in a church. It displays an institution at ease with its assumed importance. It is wholly white, middle class, and English; the accents are confident, establishment assured.

The service starts, as now, with Milner-White's moving prayer. In this service, it is read by the Provost rather than the Dean, but the Dean rounds off the service with his final blessing and prayer from the high altar, intoning between high candlesticks, darkly surrounded, all very high church. The College looks as if it would continue confidently unperturbed for decades. But yet within four months of this film, the assured opening and closing speakers were both dead. The Dean died a month later on 21 January aged 53, having returned from a visit to a College living and thrown himself off the top of the west end of his chapel. Three months after that, on April 26th, the Provost who seemed totally well on the morning of his 56th birthday, suddenly died of a massive heart attack in the Provost's Lodge.

Within the next ten years, the dark surroundings displayed in the film were torn out: the high altar was demolished, George Gilbert Scott the Younger's massive candlesticks were removed, and the comforting wooden sheathing of the Chapel's east end was carted off to moulder in a damp store. The floor was lowered with scant respect for the generations of Fellows buried beneath, who were jumbled up and carted off before the site was concreted over. It is difficult to imagine getting permission today for such a drastic change to a famous building; permission was not needed in the 1960s but people still write to the College to protest at the vandalism. The Director of Music, who is seen on the film conducting with undemonstrative authority, was already not well; within two years, he was unable to continue; within five years, he was taken down G staircase and wheeled to the Senate House to receive his honorary degree; and a year later he was also dead. So far, perhaps, so familiarly sad. But in fact the unexpected deaths of both Provost and Dean marked a significant turning point in the history of the College. With new personnel, King's once again changed and remade itself, as manifested by its dramatic assault on its most famous building.

After the Dean's sudden death, the College initially attempted to carry on with business as usual. A committee sat and identified an appropriately sound replacement, who was approached and consented to serve. But then, with the need also to find a new Provost, there was a rebellion, led as usual by the more junior Fellows. It was decided that the College wanted more than a dean who could intone amid the incense. An intellectual college should have an intellectual dean. More generally, the College was felt to be too comfy, too gentlemanly, and pay insufficient attention to science. A powerful speech by Noel Annan convinced a majority that change was needed and, once convinced, the majority voted him as Provost at the age of 39.

This was a generational revolution and Annan came in as Provost with a clear mandate for change. Nor did he disappoint. Alec Vidler, editor of *Theology*, was approached and agreed to serve as Dean; he was central in the change in religious thought in 1960s Cambridge. Scientists were recruited; the Research Centre was invented; and Senior and Admission Tutors with little respect for the College's traditions were appointed. Buildings were demolished, staircases abolished, and the white sixties monster of the Keynes Building constructed. The high table was lowered and the ends of the hall were switched. No longer, as had been the case from the foundation, did the College eat together after grace had been said by a Scholar. No longer was there a hierarchical hall, with everyone in their place at dictatorially set times. Instead, as a culinary expression of King's liberalism, each man ate his self-served buffet as and when he wished. And, as noted, the Chapel was assaulted; the dead Fellows might have slept in peace for centuries but they were disturbed by Provost Annan. He was the most successful Provost of the twentieth century. (There was considerable reconstructive vigour in the 1930s, but this was led by the First Bursar rather than the Provost.)

The male pronoun for the persons eating in the new buffet is accurate. Provost Annan might have dished the gentlemen but he did not dilute the men; the admission of women to the College had to wait for his successor, Edmund Leach. Leach was elected in 1966 and in 1967 he gave, speaking as Provost of King's, a famous series of Reith Lectures on the radio entitled 'A runaway world'. This implied that the old were out of touch, the family was finished, and seemed to place King's in the vanguard of the late 60s revolution. In fact, back in College, the Provost was considerably less radical. Nevertheless, students were admitted to the College Council (initially as observers as the Privy Council would not permit students as voting members) and these students took the lead in driving for the admission of women. Somewhat surprisingly, this became an unproblematic decision, well prepared by a mixed committee of senior and junior members whose proposals were almost unanimously accepted by the

Governing Body. Some members muttered that they didn't see what difference it would make. But it did; it destroyed almost overnight King's image as an especially homosexual college.

So, practically painlessly, runaway Leach presided over ditching five centuries of College tradition. His predecessor, Provost Annan, had a tougher time in his desire to shake up the old institution. Some of his proposed changes, such as the Chapel remodelling, were extremely hard fought. Some, such as a proposed reform of the Statutes, were not only fought but failed to carry the Governing Body. And some, such as the pronounced shift to state schools, started on his watch but were not particularly promoted by any Provost. The Chapel alteration, however, was personally promoted by Annan, assisted by the resident aesthetic mandarin, Michael Jaffé, Director of the Fitzwilliam Museum and self-appointed arbiter of College taste. The problem to be solved was provided by a large picture, Rubens' *Adoration of the Magi*, whose owner wished it to be hung in keeping with its original purpose as an altar-piece. He offered it to King's as such, where it would compete with the great east window of a different century and style, even if it could be squeezed beneath it. The College placed it temporarily on an easel in the antechapel while it scratched its collective head. The eventual result (although strongly resisted by alternative arbiters of taste such as E M Forster, then resident in College as an Honorary Fellow) was an extremely close vote at the Governing Body and the already described disturbance of the dead.

The other, and even bigger, building project of the Annan period was sweeping away the lecture block, the Drain, and the old kitchens to build (in combination with St Catharine's) the Keynes Building. The resulting building was all white, horizontal, and modern, such as Keynes himself had failed to get in the 1930s when he tried to remove the library. It runs, with a flying freehold, above the neighbouring college as a ghostly, aerial, reminder of when King's used to have rooms on the far side of King's Lane. And, by one of the ironies of history, the insalubrious underground passage of the

Drain that Keynes wished removed was replaced by the insalubrious passage of an altered King's Lane.

As we have seen, the College had already started in the twenties bringing in scientists from outside. But Annan increased the pace, particularly after his creation of the Research Centre, many of whose research groups were in the sciences. He brought in Sydney Brenner in 1958 to join Fred Sanger, who came on an external competition in 1954. Sanger stayed in his lab, concentrating on winning his second Nobel Prize. But Brenner, as well as running the Molecular Biology lab, served the College non-stop for over twenty-five years without a break as an Elector of Fellowships with persistent care for the scientific development of the College before also becoming Nobel.

The driving force for a similarly significant change in the student body was Tutors rather than Provosts. It started with John Broadbent, appointed Senior Tutor under Annan and serving from 1963 to 1968. He explicitly, brutally, and consciously cut the link with Eton. We have seen in the last chapter how the small minority of Etonian Scholars still added a distinctive intellectual presence and in 1955, the year this chapter starts, the single star first in History finals was from Eton and King's. Broadbent stopped this, sending out a shock wave not just to Eton but to the leading public schools more generally, who became markedly less enthusiastic about supplying candidates. This provided an opportunity for three successive Admission Tutors (Jim Turner, Keith Tipton, and Alan Bilsborough) to encourage more state school applicants. Inside twenty years, King's changed from being a strongly public school college to one whose students overwhelmingly came from the state sector.

This process culminated under Provost Williams (but, again, on the initiative of the Tutors) when the College decided to abolish entrance scholarships. This was a much more daring and radical step at the time than it seems in retrospect and can be compared to the admission of women some fifteen years before under Provost Leach. In making the decision unilaterally (unlike with the women, where there was co-ordination with two other colleges), King's risked completely isolating itself while the other colleges continued happily awarding scholarships and drawing away the best students. However, once again King's radicalism benignly placed the College in the van with all the other colleges coming almost immediately into line, just as they had more slowly with the admission of women. This decision was similarly surprisingly uncontentious at the Governing Body. One old Fellow got up and said that he had come to King's as an Entrance Scholar, just like all the Fellows sitting beside him. So, thought the younger hopefuls, sunk again by sentiment, memory, and tradition. Not a bit of it. "Out of date!" he roared; no point King's having entrance scholarships ever since there had been state support for students.

It was not accidental that King's was a particularly public school college in the early fifties. Unlike the other colleges, it did not use the scholarship exam for general entrance but instead had a strongly bi-focal admissions procedure. Those of scholarship level in the exam were admitted, whatever else they were like, and they maintained the College's top level results in finals, consistently throughout this decade the best of any college. However the majority of the students were admitted at the sole discretion of the Senior Tutor. From 1946 to 1956, this was Patrick Wilkinson. He interviewed boys when they were 16, much earlier than the other colleges, and offered places to those who were 'interesting'. Some got awards in the later scholarship exam, but most merely remained interesting. This early selection tended to favour the public schools (as, probably, did the requirement of being 'interesting') since the state schools thought about Cambridge later and in the context of the exam.

'Interesting' for Wilkinson tended to mean a gift for drama or journalism and fifties King's was a performing college, strongly interested in the arts. It was also Arts in its subject balance. In the mid-decade, History, Classics, and Modern Languages each had more students than read Natural Sciences; 40% of the students at King's read one of these three subjects, as compared with 25% in the University. Then Annan and Broadbent got to work, with striking results. In 1965 only 21% read these three subjects, now the same proportion as the University. Natural Sciences was now the largest subject, followed by Mathematics. History had descended to less than 9% as opposed to over 15% the decade before; King's had ceased to be what it was throughout the last chapter, a college particularly of History and Classics.

The College was also as suddenly changed in its social composition because by now frightening the public schools had produced a college of grammar school boys. This is how it is remembered by Tony Judt, who arrived in 1966 as one of the diminished Historians. Among his many friends was only one from a public school and the statistics bear out his subjective impression of how much the College had changed. The new grammar school boys felt that they owned the College as much as the Etonians ever had and Judt thought that they uniquely benefited from the mixture of continuity and change; although new style students, they were still taught by old style dons. He says that "we were never taught with the specific aim of performing well on the Tripos." This is still the style of the last chapter and Judt's own particular career would have been recognisable at any time after the 1880s reforms: although not performing particularly well in the Tripos, he was elected to a Fellowship on the strength of his dissertation and so started a successful academic career. When Judt arrived, the students wore gowns in hall and stood while the elderly dons shuffled past them before grace; they were required to be inside the locked-up college every night and had to climb in illegally if out after hours. When he graduated three years later, all this was only a quaint memory.

Even for the substantially changed students, the sixties did not particularly swing at King's although they ended with a student revolution in which the College burnished its radical credentials. King's students were prominent in the University demonstrations and planned the successful occupation of the University Senate House. (The initiating cause, hardly the stuff of government-destroying revolutions, was the status of dissertations in the Economics Tripos.)

Yet it was strangely quiet in house where the undergraduates did not occupy, or otherwise attempt to hurt, the College. Partly this was because the College had already granted natural student causes such as access to government; partly it was because of the continuing close friendship between students and dons; and partly it was because of the humanity and skill of the Senior Tutors. Here Ken Polack filled the gap until Geoffrey Lloyd could take over, having first been sent by the anthropological Provost to prepare himself by studying tribes of revolting students in their native California habitat.

The grammar schools of sixties King's had competed with the public schools in Cambridge admissions and given them a fair run in the scholarship exams. But then national and local government laid envious hands upon them. Direct Grants became independent and County Councils abolished their grammar schools; the College's new state school market had disappeared and the scholarship examination now inevitably favoured the independent sector. Its reaction, however, was not to stay with the schools that specially prepared people for Cambridge. Instead, it changed its admission system and encouraged applicants from comprehensives and other state schools previously unused to applying. By the eighties, the composition of the student body had become very like the English universities generally and very unlike the University of Cambridge.

In his book called *Our Age*, Noel Annan contrasts King's when he became Provost with thirty years later. When he (and this chapter) started, almost 70% of the entry came from public schools (and 18% of the remainder from Direct Grants). Whereas by the mid-1980s, 70% were from state schools. The second contrast he makes is that, when he was Provost, King's consistently had the best results in the University but, he notes, the very different later entry no longer produced top results. However, Annan would only have had to wait a short time for this picture to change. During the second half of the Eighties, King's was once again consistently best in the final examinations, as reported annually in the national press. With a conspicuously wider entry that nevertheless achieved conspicuously good results, something was clearly going right and College officers had the satisfaction of being invited to lunch by their opposite numbers in other colleges to discover what it was and whether it was possible to emulate it.

Good results come from good teaching of high-quality applicants and during this period both were presided over by Tess Adkins as Senior Tutor. She was appointed during the Provostship of Bernard Williams and for many who were there, the decade with Bernard as Provost and Tess as Tutor was a high point. The College was still liberal, informal, and somewhat eccentric with respect to the rest of the University. But it was also confident and successful, taking particular care with its students. During her time as Senior Tutor, King's was so secure in its ability to support troubled students that it was prepared to take the risk of admitting predictably difficult applicants (who were also predictably good) in a way that other colleges might not. Probably, this was a further factor behind the excellent results; certainly, it meant that several potential lost souls were saved by the College.

The three History Fellows who taught Tony Judt had all been undergraduates at the College and were steeped in its tradition. (Two of them, indeed, wrote the previous two short histories of the College.) However, after his time, this reproduction inside the college did not continue. The annual election of members of the College to Fellowships (through which these three had come) was stopped after a hundred years at the heart of King's. Research Fellows came from outside and the College similarly took as teachers University employees who had no previous college connection. Women were admitted at the senior level and there was a much greater diversity of nationalities and previous educational institutions in the Fellowship. Back in the 1960s, Judt had the benefit of being a new-style student taught by old-style dons but by the 1980s the dons had also become new style.

The changing dons were reflected by the changing nature of the provosts they elected. In the first half of the period described in this chapter, King's continued as before: the provosts elected were English, male, public school, from the Arts rather than the Sciences, and already Fellows of the College. But in 1988 it elected a scientist and in 2003 someone from outside the Fellowship. In 2012, the mistake made of refusing to elect Isaac Newton (Mathematical Fellow of Trinity) was remedied, a mere 323 years later, by the election of Michael Proctor (Mathematical Fellow of Trinity), the first time that a current fellow of another college was elected Provost since King's gained control.

Provosts are epiphenomena and even the composition of the Fellowship that elects them is relatively superficial when compared with the chief motor of change, which is finance. With money, we reach the real shifting tectonic plates. The simplest story of this chapter is that at its start the College was rich whereas at its end it was not. At the start, the College's assessed income for the purposes of its University Contribution, as might be expected, placed King's behind Trinity. But it was not far behind, with £129,000 to Trinity's £136,000, and three years earlier King's had been ahead of Trinity with the highest income of any college. Far below these two giants were St John's (71k) and then Caius (67k). In the next decade two Fellows (Jasper Rose and John Ziman) wrote an account of Oxford and Cambridge that they called *Camford Observed*. They append charts of the relative wealth of the colleges. Here again King's, with £191,000, is on talking terms with Trinity (249k) and still ahead of John's (147k); it is also far richer than every Oxford college.

This is the background to the College's confident aristocratic style of revolution with which this chapter started. It permitted patronage and allowed operation at a tangent to the rest of the University. It was why King's could have its own Research Centre, not used as a channel for external funding but paying instead the salaries of its research fellows as they opened up areas neglected by the University. The competition for projects (based on presentations in a large, passionate, meeting in the Provost's Drawing Room, listened to and decided on by the Centre Managers) was a competition for College resources; the money was there. If you are (and more importantly if you feel) as rich as Trinity, then you are able to act with assurance; if you are wealthier than Christ Church or Magdalen in Oxford, then you are entitled to make an intellectual splash.

A decade later (in the assessed 1974-5 accounts) John's has moved well ahead, Trinity is out of sight with twice as much, and the College has been bumped by Caius. The position is much the same after another decade. In 1985-6, King's and Caius are still roughly level, John's has 50% more, and Trinity now has an income well over three times as much as King's. The College is among the richer colleges. But it is trying to finance similar responsibilities to Trinity and John's, supporting as many research fellows as well as maintaining the local cathedral, with a relatively declining income. By the end of the 1990s the College has dropped to sixth, with not only Trinity, John's and Caius ahead but also Emma and Jesus; Trinity is now over eight times as rich. The College once grandly on terms with Trinity now had to be very humble.

When in the nineties Bursars eventually managed to make the College face up to the financial facts, it savagely cut its spending on research. There were no more exciting meetings in the Provost's Drawing Room to argue over the next Research Centre project to support and Annan's once proud centre was reduced to a name on a door with nothing behind. (Or to be completely accurate, two names on two doors as the little room opposite it remained labelled 'Research Toilet'.) Cutting research removed something important to the College's self-identity in this period; the cost of a Research Fellow was the unit of account in general financial discussion and plans were measured by their impact on research (with serious detriment to building maintenance).

Whereas previously the Electors to Fellowships and the College Council tended to be composed of the same central people, by the seventies and eighties after the Annan reforms, the Electors were a separate and superior group. It was like a little college of cardinals, election to which was keenly contested, and which contained an impressive array of fast thinking intellectual talent. (Typical Electors, like Sydney Brenner mentioned above, were Dan McKenzie and Martin Rees in science and Bernard Williams and Frank Kermode in arts.) A subset of them managed the Research Centre and the main body had the confidence to elect in all subjects without bothering external experts. Then, come the nineties, it all unravelled. The Research Centre disappeared and the number of other elections was drastically reduced. The Electors were abolished and replaced by a Research Committee; eventually research was thought to be of so little importance that this committee was no longer chaired by the Provost and the serene confidence of the departed mandarins was replaced by impotent ill-tempered argument.

Given that the College was self-confidently successful in the mid-eighties but was struggling by the mid-nineties, it is tempting to look more precisely for a point of transition. A natural one to select is the election of Pat Bateson as Provost in 1987, if only because it was a traumatic event to those who lived through it (and who were so subsequently obsessed by it that Fellows arriving later begged them to stop talking about it.) If an election goes wrong, as this one clearly did in its process if not in its result, it damages the confidence of the College. Something similar, although less severely, happened in 2011 when the College advertised for a new Provost, interviewed candidates and fixed the date for election in Chapel, but failed to achieve a result. This was bad and caused lasting damage. But the 1987 election has no parallel in the College's sudden descent from confidence to a cataclysm of angry recrimination. The formal vote in Chapel was so close that a single person voting differently would have led to a different result. This alone would have required unusual sensitivity. But what mainly caused the problem was that on the morning of the election, after months devoted to discussion, the winning camp sent to selected Fellows material designed to belittle the rival candidate, which his supporters had no opportunity to rebut. This was widely felt to be dishonourable and what made it worse was that, with only a single Fellow needing to be turned, it might well have been successfully dishonourable. Hence the subsequent descent into fury, which meant that the new Provost, though no fault of his own, inherited a college that was initially ungovernable.

Like purely monetary effects in economics, this is only important for how it affected Fellows' feelings. It was a valid election, which produced a Provost who did the job and who might safely have been elected by an honourable process. If any deeper significance can be divined, then perhaps the instant anthropological analysis of Edmund Leach is as good as any. The thirteen most senior Fellows voted for Bateson and Leach was in fact the first Fellow in the descending hierarchical order who voted against him. Coming out of the Chapel after the election, he declared that those who had voted for Bateson wore ties and those who voted against him did not. (It should be remembered that this was a time when many more men wore ties and when in any other college every man would have worn a tie at a formal occasion of this importance.) This echoes the cultural conflict between the best set and the excluded in the 1880s, which was sometimes similarly sartorially expressed. A group of self-declared outsiders in University terms, with an alternative egalitarian ideology, thought that at least they were at home in King's but to their surprise (and subsequent fury) discovered that this was not quite correct. Even at King's the suits won, as they always do.

In 1987 the College sleepwalked into sudden chaos and the unexpected self-inflicted wound tended to bestow retrospective allure on the period immediately before, which became in memory the steadily sunlit philosophical reign of Provost Williams. But in fact, just as in other periods, Williams had problems. He presided with great style and sparkle. But he started with a nasty rent strike which he couldn't resolve; the students were impervious to his charm and bricks were thrown through the windows of the Provost's Lodge. Twice he attempted to build a new College library. Expensive architects were engaged and plans were prepared, once to bisect Webb's Court and once in the Fellows' Garden. The First Bursar assured the Fellowship that the money was there but they nevertheless defeated both proposals. By this measure, Provost Bateson was a success where Provost Williams was not. Bateson built a new Garden Hostel near where Williams had failed to build his library and constructed a new court in King's Parade by raising a plinth at the back to which each house became a staircase.

With finance already in decline, the 1987 election was a mere blip on the underlying real process and whoever won was going to have a harder time. We have seen how it cost the College its prime and prestigious institute of advanced studies. But it also slipped back on areas not so immediately financially sensitive. It lost its other research institute, the self-funded Centre of History and Economics, when it transferred to a more congenial college. Its lead in attracting the best state school candidates was eroded as other colleges moved into the market and the University was leant on by the Government to widen access. The King's admissions operation became less distinctive. The College's results descended from best to average, partly because of increased competition for state school candidates and partly because Fellows became less committed to teaching.

Thirty years of financial pressure did not however inhibit all activity. The College steadily renewed its hostel accommodation. It managed again to increase its support of research so that the Research Committee, once more chaired by the Provost, recovered some of the momentum and morale of the old Electors. It took another initiative in admissions, opening a new front in continental Europe so that a quarter of undergraduates came from the non-British EU. As compared with the male, white, middle class English undergraduates at the start of the chapter, the student body has been totally transformed. The graduates were always international, but the undergraduates are now very much more varied. So also for the Fellows: they are similarly almost unrecognisably different in character from the white male Englishmen with which this chapter started. Constantly changing in their composition, they are unburdened by history. We have seen through the last two chapters how the College has constantly reinvented itself. Each time it did, it had to work through and against its previous history. But now the College is no longer constrained by history and is ripe without resistance for its next reinvention.

And so this story reaches its end. This could be because we have boringly run into the buffers of the present. Or it might more excitingly be because the College's history has itself ended in the sense that it is no longer the case that anything about its unusual past explains anything about its actual present. In my view, the end is still partially boring. Many once familiar landmarks have been dissolved and the College is less constrained by the dead hand of history than it has ever been. But its unusual history does, I think, still effectively explain the current college in two important aspects.

Ever since the nineteenth century reforms, the power in King's has been with the Governing Body. Other colleges creating councils in the 1880s made them general purposes executive committees acting on behalf of their Fellowships; King's considered this but did not do it, making instead Education the Council's particular responsibility. Other central areas such as Research, Investment, Finance, and Buildings have been considered by committees reporting directly to the Governing Body and Fellows at the Governing Body have felt free to dispense with proposals, whatever their origin. King's is therefore an unusual direct democracy, similar to Classical Athens, with power in the hands of the Fellowship as a whole. It is an oral culture, where Fellows of equal standing make speeches; some speak much more than others but the majority decides, even if it means following the rhetoric and ignoring the carefully prepared plans of the College Officers. Provosts and Bursars at King's ride a tiger with occasional uncertainty over direction of travel and the constant possibility of being eaten.

This rich and thriving democratic culture is in continuity with the College's past, is explained by it, and still makes King's distinctively different from other Cambridge colleges. New Fellows can see it on entry, understand it, and in due course continue its operation. Maynard Keynes was responsible for many aspects of twentieth century King's and among them was the Junior Caucus. When he was a young Fellow, he invited the other young Fellows to meet together to discuss business coming to the Annual Congregation and so invented the still existing Junior Caucus. With its help, he succeeded in defeating the First Bursar's proposals. In turn, as we saw in the last chapter, Keynes himself as First Bursar was defeated in his building proposals by junior Fellows. Whether by Caucus or otherwise, it is the Fellows who have the power. The College was privileged to have one of the best economists in the world as its Bursar in the 1930s and privileged to have one of the best Moral Philosophers in the world as its Provost in the 1980s. Yet neither of these supremely clever gentlemen could persuade the Governing Body to build a library.

The other element in which the College maintains continuity with its past and has not exhausted its cultural capital is the Chapel. The most prominent and most successful survivor of the centuries surveyed in this short history, it's where the present college can only be made sense of in terms of its past. Someone today removing the centre of Cambridge to construct a college would not produce one with this balance of buildings or functions. The waves of change may wash away other landmarks but they beat in vain against the great cliff of the Chapel. Beautifully maintained in its external structure, it links the current college back to its foundation and the plans of its saintly founder. All has not been serene inside; there has been fiddling with the furnishing and the unfortunate suicide of a Dean at the beginning of this chapter was matched by the unfortunate suicide of another Dean near its end. Yet the Chapel persists unchanged not only in external fabric but also in internal function, performing the same process as it has for hundreds of years. The Choir, like the Governing Body, has an established tradition, which is seen and understood by new entrants who in turn reproduce it. The Founder's Statutes said that there should be sixteen choristers to sing the daily services and anyone looking inside the immobile cliff of the Chapel will still see sixteen sweetly singing.

Michaelmas 2014

And with thanks to…

Mike Proctor, the Provost, initiated the process and advised me to cheer up the concluding chapter. Peter Jones, the Fellow Librarian, was a constant source of help, including reading depressing drafts and checking the completed work. Patricia McGuire, the College Archivist, opened up, explained, and helped me negotiate the College Archives. The content of the last chapter is all within living memory and I was here helped by those of John Dunn and Geoffrey Lloyd. None of them is responsible for any of the foregoing but I am grateful for their help. RH

APPENDIX

PROVOSTS OF KING'S COLLEGE

Name	Appointed
William Millington	1441
John Chedworth	1447
Robert Wodelark	1452
Walter Field	1479
John Dogget	1499
John Argentine	1501
Richard Hatton	1508
Robert Hacomblen	1509
Edward Fox	1528
George Day	1538
John Cheke	1549
Richard Atkinson	1553
Robert Brassie	1556
Philip Baker	1558
Roger Goad	1570

Fogge Newton	1610
William Smith	1612
Samuel Collins	1615
Benjamin Whichcote	1645
James Fleetwood	1660
Thomas Page	1676
John Coplestone	1681
Charles Roderick	1689
John Adams	1712
Andrew Snape	1720
William George	1743
John Sumner	1756
William Cooke	1772
Humphrey Sumner	1797
George Thackeray	1814
Richard Okes	1850
Augustus Austen Leigh	1889
Montague Rhodes James	1905
Walter Durnford	1918
Alan Brooke	1926
John Sheppard	1933
Stephen Glanville	1954
Noel Annan	1956
Edmund Leach	1966
Bernard Williams	1979
Patrick Bateson	1988
Judith Mayhew Jonas	2003
Ross Harrison	2006, 2011
Michael Proctor	2013